FREE F

MENTAL SLAVERY

Volume 2

BY

PASEKA S. MAZIBUKO - ZIBU 4

Bhiyoza PUBLISHERS

Bhiyoza Publishers (Pty) Ltd

FREE PEOPLE FROM MENTAL SLAVERY

Volume 2

Bhiyoza Publishers (Pty) Ltd

Johannesburg, South Africa

Bhiyoza Publishers (Pty) Ltd
PO Box 1139
Ridgeway
2099

Email: info@bhiyozapublishers.co.za
www.bhiyozapublishers.co.za

First edition, first impression 2020
ISBN: 978-1-990988-70-7
Cover design: Yanga Graphix (Pty) Ltd
Layout and typeset: Yanga Graphix (Pty) Ltd

Table of contents

FOREWORD

"People will never change but they can change their ways, their mental thinking and mute the old ways" ~ Paseka Simon Mazibuko

This book, ***FREE PEOPLE FROM MENTAL SLAVERY,*** written by ***Mr Simon Mazibuko*** from ***Tshiame in Harrismith (Free State Province: South Africa)*** is based on a true story experienced by the author in his life. This book is all about changing or emancipating the inner game. Through the publication of his book, he worked with ***Mr Mokgasi Paka Duma Blackcat Mosia (Author and Director of DL Mosia Blackcat Literary Club (Pty) Ltd)*** who is also under ***Mr Paseka Simon Mazibuko a.k.a Zibu4***'s mentorship. He was apprehended and sentenced to three years' imprisonment for a crime he did not commit. His legal proceeding was unfairly litigated. He was not assumed to be innocent until proven guilty; instead, he was found guilty based on hearsay prior to court proceedings. He was not given a chance to state his side of the story and his conviction negatively affected his life, profession, and his occupation as a teacher. His character and reputation were tainted in toto. It separated him from his family and his parents passed away while he was in prison for a crime he did not commit.

This book is a motivation to those who want to be freed from mental slavery and to those who refuse to be freed from mental slavery by encouraging them to submit themselves to this emancipation of the mind. To change, have a new mentality, as well as physical and mental wealth.

He was betrayed,
But he made it,
He was heartbroken,
But he made it,
He was unfairly treated,
But he made it,
He was impoverished,
But he made it,

He was rejected,

But he made it,

Because he believed that: "***GREAT INNOVATIONS ARE BUILT ON REJECTION" ~ Paseka Simon Mazibuko***

God bestowed him with blessings for serving the universe with his emancipated mind. This book is not written based on theory but on experience and can positively influence and change the mindset of people. It was not written to entertain but to make the world a better place inhabited by people who are the change they wish to see in life. The contents of this book need time to be properly digested and should be adopted by all.

I HOPE IT WILL FREE YOU FROM MENTAL SLAVERY...

ABOUT THE AUTHOR

Paseka. S. Mazibuko is from Tshiame A, Harrismith, in the Eastern Free State. He was born and bred at the township known as Intabazwe in Harrismith in the Free State Province. He attended schooling at Vulindlela Primary School early seventies where he completed standard two.

He was the Captain the first division of the school's soccer team under Principalship of Mrs Mfusi on the year 1976 - 1977. He then went to Intabazwe Higher Primary School on the year 1978 and completed standard five on the year 1980.

On the year 1981 - 1985 he attended school at Harrismith Senior Secondary School where he completed Matric/ Standard ten.

On the year 1987 he attended Tshiya College of Education in QwaQwa where he completed his Senior Teachers Diploma on the year 1989. He specialized in

Afrikaans and Biblical Studies and his Ancillary subject was Physical Training.

On the year 1990 he started teaching at Sasamala Secondary School in Tshiame A up until the year 2012 and that is where he was falsely accused of attempted rape to his Grade ten class learner as he was her class teacher that year, of which this story is all about.

Currently he is a teacher and motivator working at home by helping in the township and around with English, Afrikaans and other subjects as requested by the parents and the community at large. He is also an author - writing books as this first one and the next one which is in the pipeline entitled "Church of Churchless".

DEDICATION

This book and its message is dedicated to those oppressed by their own ignorance and greed.

In commemoration of my beloved deceased mother, Ms. Evelina Nomalanga Dlamini, who passed away whilst I was imprisoned in the year 2015, September 20th. May her soul rest in peace.

THANKS TO:

My wife, Bella Mazibuko, my family, learners, colleagues, and friends.

ACKNOWLEDGEMENTS

With deep gratitude, I acknowledge my deceased parents "May their souls rest in peace" for the profound influence on my life and on my thinking.

I also acknowledge many authors of different books, thought leaders, philosophers ... living or dead. Some of whom I do not remember as well their books' titles for instance Encyclopaedia I read whilst behind bars. Some of whom are referenced throughout the book, for their influence on my thinking and on the development of this book. This book could not have been written without their help. I am deeply thankful.

To my wife, Bella M. Mazibuko and daughter Nonhlanhla A. Mazibuko, for their constant encouragement, unbelievable kindness, and abundant trust.

Most importantly, I acknowledge and thank God for the blessings, insights, and support I have felt when writing this book. For me, He is the source of all principles that bring joy and success in life.

CHAPTER 1

HEALING RELATIONS IN MARRIAGES

Displaced guilt on the other hand is that feeling of guilt that is detached from the original idea and appears in the individual's awareness as a different idea such as remorse over some small act or a haunting fear that he or she has done something reprehensible like injuring someone with his or her car.

Normal or Healthy guilt furthermore in the mature adult becomes a feeling of having violated the integrity of the self-system; a feeling of self - hostility for not achieving the ideal of the self - image and the habit of obedience in the adult gives way to self - guidance based on a broad schemata of values that confer direction upon conduct, therefore learning from past experiences become blended with present experiences so that one's ethical sensitivity is sharpened and one's level of insight is deepened.

Conscience connotes three quite different things which are inventory submission to external authorities with the concomitant fear of discovery and punishment. Condemnatory self - accusation and discontent with self in a constructive sense. According to Freudian view, conscience is considered a learned concept arising largely out of internalisation; parental prohibitions; threats and values.

These internalized values are picked up through the process of incidental learning during early childhood and punishment rather than rewards which seem to be the decisive determinants. According to his framework, personality problems are caused by a severe superego overwhelming the ego and forcing it to repress the biologically based primitive impulses of the id.

Mowrer on the other side claims that disturbances in personality are caused by the id and the ego by joining forces against superego and that the ego functions are immature and under the influence of the id and have done things of which the superego disapproves.

He further indicates that the person with a diminutive superego and an immature ego would tend toward antisocial criminal acts whereas the person with the over developed superego would lead to over socialization and rigid, which would place severe demands on the ego and restraint on the id.

As the child grows, parental demands become internalized into feelings of rightness and wrongness. As he or she grows into adolescence, he or she acquires a self - picture as a moral person with the mores a part of his or her basic value system. This value system is based on earlier learned values which is a growing self - awareness and rationally determined view of the mores.

A humanistic view is based on the fact that if the child grows up feeling that conscience is somehow absolute and synonymous with divine or cosmic law. The child may go through life trying to live up to these expectation; justifying his or her actions and forever feeling guilty that he or she should be doing something he or she isn't doing or not doing something he or she is doing, but conscience can be a positive creative force in interpersonal relationships as well as inhibiting guilt provoking force.

All of what I experienced ; discovered and learnt has made me realise that the dual task of the Counsellor is to help the person to develop a stronger ego that is able to escape control by the id and to develop a working relationship with the superego . Many people try to do what someone else is good at instead of doing what they are good at. Unfortunately, most people don't take the time to ask themselves: "Why they do what they do?" Is it because God is said to be less concerned or impressed by what we do than why we do it?

When we submit to God, we are sowing seeds of obedience that will bring a wonderful harvest in our lives hence each time I have ignored the inside information to avoid being sorry later. Therefore, I plan and execute my first failure so that I no longer have to fear it. James 4 - 6 says: "Pray and Ask Him to show us a plan for each day and begin to work the plan." Waking up each morning and knowing that we were born for this day, that we are living in the purpose of God and are part of the great adventure of expanding His Kingdom here on earth as it is in heaven.

God has given us hopes and dreams to pursue our whole hearts. The problem is that many of us have the passion to see the things we hope for to become reality but has to be buried and we have given in to hopelessness when it seemed, like our dreams would never become reality.

In my understanding we were created to live with purpose and passion. It is what gets us up and keep us going each day. God has placed in each of us a strong desire to reach for something beyond ourselves which is a natural longing to reach for the goals that are unreachable apart from His help. We were created to enjoy God and do His will because He is the Alpha and Omega - the Beginning and the End, therefore He must also be everything in between.

Knowing and understanding our purpose is the first step toward doing all God has planned for us. When we understand our purpose, it becomes a road map guiding us toward our destiny in Christ. In my understanding, Passion is that keeps us going on our journeys. It is therefore vital that we keep an ample supply, and we should constantly be experiencing the life of God Who does everything passionately and with purpose with His whole heart.

Well, ladies and gentlemen, let me clarify my role with you. You might say I wear two coats around here of which are my Teacher's coat and my counsellor's coat. When I wear my teacher's coat, I have to be evaluating and judging to a certain degree in order to state your progress as my student. When I see people personally in a relationship such as this, I have encountered and experienced in my life, then I am wearing my counsellor's coat. This means that you can feel free to talk about anything you like, and I will not hold it against you or make judgements about you. OK?

In my research and study, I discovered that the aim of Counselling is to create self - direction in people. As a Counsellor I realised that, when I concentrate on the individual's feelings rather than the ideal and content of his or her remarks, I will be reaching the individual at a deep motivational level. I also realised that, by working together I think that we can arrive at some answers for us both especially you so as to understand what I think about life and my current situation.

I discovered that if the person feels exploited and abused, I as a Counsellor should be careful in making demands upon him or her but if the person's former human relationships have been characterized by rejection or devaluation then I should be very accepting and warm.

I learnt that, marital counselling is tied to the Therapeutic Psychology and that Social Workers analyse the total family situation. Such Professionals have worked mainly in Agencies with low - income clients. They therefore have begun to develop service designed for the middle-income clients.

Stone is said to have established the first marriage consultation Centre in New York in the year 1929. He was followed by "Popenoe "who is said to have established the Institute of Family Relations in the year 1930 and it is said much pioneer work has been done by Emily Mudd since 1932 when she established the Philadelphia Marriage Council.

It is said there were two Organisations dedicated to professionalizing this field of which were the American Association of Marriage Counsellors and the National Council on Family Relations. The Clergy has been associated with marital counselling particularly pre- marital counselling and the family Physician played a particular role in pre - marital counselling but it is said that the professional Medical men were involved in the establishment of healthy attitudes toward sex and contraception and the Lawyer's special role in relation to accepting or rejecting divorces because of their highly specialized area of Legal information and rules which makes them an important partner in marital counselling .

The Courts on the other hand were paying increasing attention to the part they can play in bringing about reconciliation rather than granting divorce but today especially here in Ebumnandini our Courts are turning things upside down as they don't give a damn about people's marital or work issues as it seems to them they are satisfied to destroy people's lives instead of building by using their so-called laws which are enforced to people like myself who is a layman and knows nothing about laws and legal procedure and so on hence men end up putting forth statements to the wives like for instance:" Who died and made you the head of this house?"

Judge Louis Burke founded the Conciliation Court in Los Angeles in which Psychologists and Social Workers gave reconciliation counselling wherein the Psychologists were applying their psychotherapeutic techniques and making special applications to the field of marriage and legal problems in their private practices.

There is no one best way to solve marital difficulties hence marital Psychotherapy usually requires that the Therapist begin with the individual Spouses themselves and their unique problems. The marriage Therapist works with the individual first and then with the relationship. A couple may be helped to live together in relative harmony and security even though the goal of a close marriage tie is impossible.

Divorce is not the costliest experience possible to a child because unhappy marriage without divorce which is an emotional divorce can be far more destructive to the child than divorce hence one of the most common considerations in divorce is the effect it will have on the children involved. My advice to the child or children of estranged parents is that they should know that they are not to blame ; that their parents will love them; that something is wrong but not as they fear everything and that their parents are not gods but humans too who have made mistakes.

I discovered that the basic problem of many marital conflicts is the lack of a healthy self - regard in one or both partners. Infidelity is often a symptom of not having achieved this major therapeutic goal of self - actualisation. In such conflicts you'll find that the typical Spouse not feeling a sense of personal worth of love from husband or wife then seeks to prove that he or she is lovable by engaging in an extra marital affair but to simply eliminate the third person in the triangle does not help.

Let me cite some reasons based on my understanding why the wife or a woman feels to act in the way of infidelity quite apart from genuine hurt about the breach of confidence. One, it may have hurt her pride that her husband or man could be attached to anyone but herself.Two, it may be intolerable to her that her husband or man could slip out from her control and domination and the incident may have touched off a dread of desertion. She may be discontented with the marriage for reasons ofwhich she is not aware, and she may use this conspicuous occurrence as an excuse for expressing all her repressed grievance by engaging merely in an unconscious campaign of revenge. Finally, she may have felt attracted toward another man and resent the fact that her husband or man indulged in a freedom that she had not allowed herself.

I have also realised that there are several deep characterological problems that often are seriously aggravated by marriage of which are Alcoholism, gambling, extreme jealousy, compulsive nagging, chronic complaining and violent temper. It then came to my attention that moralistic admonitions to do the "Right thing" will not help these individuals.

In my understanding the marital Therapy causes the marital relationship to get worse rather than better because Therapy brings to consciousness hostile feelings of which many have remained dormant for years and for the fact that many mate choices are based on some form of neurotic attraction and couples develop insight into the personality; feelings and the behaviour of his or her mate by having empathy for his or her mate.

Marriage appears doomed unless mutual empathy can be developed because when empathy is not experienced, an individual often feels that there is no basis for the relationship and do not consider the fact that you get worse before you get better.

Having received an empathy response, a person may be more ready to show empathy for others hence empathy is one of four many bases of building confidence and security in a marriage because without empathy there can be little basic acceptance between human beings.

Let me differentiate between Empathy and Sympathy so that it could be easier for a reader to understand the difference between the two in any relationships or marriage. Empathy is a direct apprehension of the state of mind of another person without feeling as that other person does. Sympathy on the other hand is a shared attitude which is the chief matter. Therefore, growth of empathy between husband and wife can be a measure of improvement in the marriage relationship.

I also learnt that the poor communication becomes a focal point of many quarrels because communication is a practical means for alleviating the loneliness that so many people feel in our Society but bear in mind that practical steps to improve communication do not obviate the need for emotional insight. Therefore, accurate communication in a marriage not only reduce hostility based upon misunderstanding but it can also be a basis for developing a feeling of closeness or oneness within the marriage.

Learning to value differences is a measure of personal and marital maturity hence each human being must learn to accept and develop his or her own sex role in relation to his or her past experiences; his or her present situation and his or her future goals. Each individual needs to recognize that his or her mate has different needs; that he or she has had different experiences and of necessity looks life differently and reacts to life's demands in a different manner.

I have discovered that women operate in terms of the "Eros" principle and are basically feeling or intuitive in the approach to life whilst we men operate on the "Logos" principle and tend to be more intellectual; systematic and power - centred in our approach due to the fact of basic character difference of which are masculine character for instance penetration; guidance; activity; discipline and adventurousness. The feminine character on the other hand is productive; receptiveness; protection; realism; endurance and motherliness. To complete a human relationship, Biological desire must be joined with love.

The strategy a person can follow in improving communication is to repeat what the first person says by trying to replace it by your words. A person should learn to recognize that people express themselves differently for instance, some people express affection or any other emotion by words whilst others by behaviour therefore just because something isn't expressed verbally doesn't mean it isn't felt.

People must also learn to reduce generalities to a minimum for instance you'll hear people say: "All men make life miserable for their wives." but they should state their feelings clearly first before expecting your partner to express his or her feelings by saying for instance: "I think we ought to ..." We should learn to distinguish the situation from the person by saying: "I would like to talk to you longer, but I have someone waiting for me at home." We should also learn to set aside time for communication regularly even when there is no problem to resolve by getting communication habit and to let good communication be a preventative measure to head off incipient problem.

I realised that disagreement is only symptomatic of a poor relationship. Couples with a marriage problem are often in trouble legally as well as psychologically due to the following problems I discovered in consensus in marriage of which one is finances more especially when finances are handled immaturely; social life due to social aims; job pressure as a result of dead end; wrong type of work; extra marital relationship caused by the puzzle like for instance: "Is he or she overly hostile or overly forgiving?"

Sexual conflict and sexual maladjustment is often merely symptomatic ; Different cultural backgrounds as part of defiance is the original choice of each other ; Parent - child relationships with disagreement in regard to discipline ; In - laws if they are a problem or negative attitude towards them ; In - family triangle when one partner has close ties with someone else in the family because of possessiveness ; Inadequate self – actualization for instance : "Does he or she really want to help him or herself ?" or "Does he or she want some magic solution ?" Finally, religion and life values can also be used to cover up for the differences.

As a therapist, you do not tell the couple how to run their lives because you do not function as an arbitrator by telling the couple who is right and who is wrong. As a therapist, you play no favourites as did the so-called arbitrators in my so-called Unnatural Sexual Offence case which has no concrete evidence by using hearsays witnesses and flimsy evidence just to punish me and my family for the crime I did not commit. Therapist does not place a blame but he or she helps them to understand how others have solved similar problems. Having worked through the unexpressed and unrecognised dependencies, the relationship improves a great deal. The Therapist or Counsellor often deal with the Spouse not involved in the infidelity and Referrals in marital counselling should be well informed about the problem and have direct contact with if needs be.

Why are our labour and court not following the same procedure instead of boasting by dismissing and imprisoning even the Innocents like myself just to gain whatever they gain and destroy the country as a whole for instance look at overcrowding in our so-called correctional centres and how much money does our current government spend for each inmate per year . *Wo! Hhe*! In the Apartheid era, there were no such things we are experiencing today as our prisons no longer have that dignity; inmates destroyed even after they served their punishment with the Stigma of Criminal Records. Where is our country - South Africa going? Why don't they want to learn about how other countries all over the world deal about such matters?

Separation in my point of view is the only means by which a marriage can be saved. Sometimes a separation is a necessary transition to final divorce. It is seldom instigated by the Counsellor or Therapist because transference feelings have their roots in the person's life experience hence a guy or lady with no respect could get ideas as others have enough charm to calm a snake.

For me, marriage between healthy; self-actualising people is a merging of feelings and intellectual choices which are felt to be right. Oh my God! Faulty sex Education and not carefully used sex Manuals then the approach can be grossly misleading or unhealthy even sex attitudes learned in childhood are frequent sources of trouble. Have you experienced dismissal; retrenchment; suicidal thought and depression in any way as I felt? Thanks to God, I am soul precious. Before a person can commit him or herself in marriage, Did he or she asked him or herself the following question: "What is this woman or man like?" or "What is the personality of this woman or man?"

Love involves learning to give and to receive love. The needs of the other must be at least as important as one's own otherwise mature love does not exist. Mature love requires spaces in your togetherness by standing together but not too near, for the Pillars of the Temple stand apart just like the oak tree and the Cypress grow not in each other's shadow.

I discovered that there are four basic elements of mature love of which are: The active concern for the life and growth of that which we love; Responsibility for the needs, physical and psychic of the other; Respect for the other with the ability to see a person as he or she is and to be aware of his or her unique individuality; Knowledge of self, of the other and the nature of love.

To love someone because you need him or her is "Neurotic" but to need him or her because you love him or her is "Healthy". I discovered that in our lives we have common types of Neurotic attraction of which are for instance , when one aggressive and sadistic versus one dependent and submissive; the one who is self - sufficient through emotional detachment versus one demanding love; We have also one who is neurotically ill versus the one who is extremely considerate; One with fluctuating helplessness and assertiveness versus one fluctuating in responsibility and disappointment desire for love and finally mutual attempt at domination.

Love in this sense is both an emotional feeling and a decision therefore it must not be regarded as solely one or the other. The Neurotic individual often seeks to establish intimacy with another by sexual contact rather than through a gradual association. Experiences of sudden intimacy are usually short - lived and unsatisfying because sexual desire is often mistaken with love. Frequently sexual desire is motivated by other neurotic needs of which are anxiety of aloneness; the wish to conquer or to be conquered; vanity and the wish to hurt or even to destroy.

I therefore suggest that each individual must discover what love means and how he or she can become lovable and loving in his or her own way because love of a person implies not the possession of that person but the affirmation of that person which simple means to grant him or her gladly the full right to his or her unique manhood or womanhood.

Romantic love on the other hand has cultural roots in the olden days but it survives in the present and nurtured by an endless barrage of fairy tales told in Myriads of slightly different forms in Movies; Magazines; Televisions and Novels.

Caring on the other side is expressed as a way of manifesting love and mature love comes only after a knowledge of and experience with the loved partner, but it may follow a period of disillusionment associated with romantic love. I discovered that one falls out of love because one does not work through the period of disillusionment to a new conception of love based not on projected needs but on realistic appraisal of one another and a deep valuing of each other as unique persons.

Counterfeit love on the far left can be recognised when the relationship is degrading; exploitative; possessive; violent; anti-social; irresponsible; sadistic or masochistic. In my understanding, love between man and woman is a relationship in which each helps the other to preserve and enlarge the life of the other. Love in my point of view gives naught but itself and takes naught but from itself in other words Love possesses not nor would be possessed, for love is sufficient unto love.

We are to live a passionate life, but we must first understand the difference between passion and obligation. We do what we want from passion, but we do what we must, from the sense of obligation. It was passion that motivated me to ask my lovely and beautiful wife - Belah out on a date. No one forced me to do it. I was fuelled by the force of passion and it worked because I did not only get a date with her, I got an honest; God's send and true wife as a proof that you do what you want from passion therefore we should not settle for a mere existence but to pursue the passionate; abundant life that Jesus came to give us.

I agree with the fact that some things in life start out as a passion but end up by becoming a boring obligation; that faith starts with passion and then becomes a ritual; that marriages begin with passion and become a boring routine and the ministry starts with passion and ends up as an obligation hence Paul wrote, whatever you do, do it heartily. This applies to every area of our lives including those things we are not gifted to do meaning those things we are commanded to do and for those things we are called to do.

I strongly believe that, when we live with passion, we honour God powerfully because He created us with passion and loves us with a passion. If we are to reflect the image of our Creator, we ought to be passionate people. Some of us are only passionate about spiritual matters like Churches; Bible Studies or Christian events but not about our families; marriages; work; leisure or hobbies.

Yes! It is wonderful to be passionate about our spiritual lives, but something is wrong if that is the only area where passion is applied. We can look great on the outside but if we are worried and anxious on the inside, we are not glorifying God.

The wide – open spacious life that Paul speaks about in 2 Corinthians 6 :11 -13 can only be fuelled by the force of passion because it is internally regulated by the Spirit of God and not externally motivated by events or circumstances hence every man dies but not every man really lives . The passion I am talking about is the way you and I approach life but not sexual intimacy or bursts of emotions that come and go. It is time to forsake hopelessness and unbury old hopes and dreams.

Yes! It is time to determine that we will fulfil the purpose God has for us and do it passionately and believe God to fill us with His zeal to walk in the plans He has for us by enjoying everyday life. I therefore encourage you and I to pursue being all we can be to draw closer to God and discover our specific calling in life. Once we know it; stay focused; give ourselves to our gifts and do it passionately.

We should be like an Olympic Athlete who has an inner force of passion that gives him or her to sacrifice; stay focused and stay committed. It is passion that motivates an Athlete to get out of bed and train when everyone else is asleep because passion drives us to a disciplined life. While one person hesitates because he feels inferior, the other is busy making mistakes and becoming superior hence my destiny is to do more; teach more and reach more people.

Unless one educates his/her emotions, they deteriorate to the level of beasts hence for me laughter promotes good temper, enlivens the heart, and brightens the intellects. There is no comparison between that which is lost by not succeeding and that which is lost by not trying hence laughter is the fast and the last sunshine that visits the heart and it costs nothing, comes at the call and leaves a bright spot behind. E.W. Cole once said: "It is better to laugh at the follies of mankind than to weep at them. "Time for me is the father of discovery hence I discovered that the home is a woman's most challenging and fertile field.

Time is an unfathomable secret to him or her who is always in a rush just like a man who left one woman often ended up with another one, very similar.

CHAPTER 2

WHAT A HATEFUL PLACE AM I LIVING IN?

Should I give up a dream to find happiness? I think fulfilling dreams and being happy can go together. What is it about me, have I got pimples or bad breath? You hate my jokes, I have been trying to be nice and friendly or Am I full of life and warmth, laughter spilling out of my pores, smiles filling the air around? We Fathers never want little girls to grow up and we certainly do not want to think of them in bed with a man.

In my point of view, woman has been admitted to a higher privilege than man. It has not been given to man to be the Father of God but to woman it has been given to be God's Mother. The Kingdom of God is not made of popes, bishops, monks, priests, Deacons and so on because God on the day of judgement would not ask a man, why he or she had not been a Pope or Pastor … but why we had not honour and obey Him.

The world could give me nothing which I learnt to desire and take nothing from me which I care to lose. Charity in the heart; truth in the tongue; chastity in the body are the virtues which God demands. Wo He! I have discovered that a river Diamond is the purest and the whitest of all and that Diamonds have invisible lines that hold it together which needs a special knife to cut. The parts which cracks and other flaws that keep it from being beautiful can be cut away and end up with the diamond that is pure all the way through and has pretty shape.

Facets are side grounds of diamond and they are polished, and they are the faces of gems. Each Facet catches the light from one mirror and shoots it to the others, but each mirror must be angled just right or it won't shoot the light back, but it will swallow it up.

One cut, one clean cleavage along the grain before grinding and polishing. When it comes to cleaving, a diamond is unforgiving. Either it is done perfectly or is ruined as there is no middle ground, the cleaving mallet

From childhood's hour I have not been as others were; I have not seen as others saw and I could not bring my passion from a common spring but I devoted my life to my profession as a Teacher.

How I suffer these days! What have I done to deserve this? Not a day of health and not a ray of hope! Save me! Oh, the pain of it! I languish in chains!

Is this my reward? Have I prayed in vain and doomed to long years of suffering which will lead to a painful death? Spare me! Be merciful! OH! Lord, my Almighty, my Saviour.

I believe that if a man had been good, he deserved to be honoured but if he had been a Sinner, there is more reason to help him or her. There was probably something more in my case than appears on the surface but those afflicted ones like myself are the flowers of Paradise; Pearls in the Coronet of the Eternal King waiting for the coming of the Lord Who in His Own time would change our forlorn bodies into the likeness of His Own Glory.

I know some people may take me for a ghost if it suits their convenience, though I do not consider it very polite of them. Anyone, ghost, or no ghost. I am tired of sitting down. I must stretch my hands and legs because every cloud has its sunny side. A difficulty arose where I least expected as I was hurt as well as offended, but pepper is not more biting than I can be, and I often fly out for small causes but they take me as they find me.

What a hateful place am I living in! It fills my lungs with bad air, and I toss about my bed at night and wake up with a headache every morning. I am always thinking, why not clear out of this noisome, rowdy hole? I do not suppose I shall get over this most odious and ghastly experience I ever had if I live.

I would rather face the pains than encounter them again because my mind was unaffected. The devil had me at advantage in my sleep. The angel of darkness trying all his or her allurements to tempt my conscience into acquiescence in evil but I believe in God Who tempers His anger with compassion for instance When He drove Adam and Eve from Paradise , He at least gave them a coat of skins . Even Christ had left Heaven and came to Earth for Sinner's Souls hence the foundation would not flourish if it is built upon injustice as the angels of darkness almost made a beggar of me.

My conscience says, I ought to be thankful to God for given me a family and the wife that is not like theirs.

My conscience says, it is a blessing because I am spared, mercy and a providential escape plus a warning. My conscience also tells me to write and tell you exactly about my life whilst in Prison although it will take me an awfully long time to do so but I prefer to tell you all about it face to face if our paths cross again in happier circumstances .

Did you know that the name Margaret comes from the Greek word “Margaron” which means “Pearl”? While the so-called Margarets are young and beautiful, that is the time they can make men love them and have anything they want because there is nothing like money for keeping one alive to ripe old age hence it is embarrassing for men to be staring at the man’s daughter like a dog with its tongue hanging out and their income stretched to the limit because they were seized at that moment by a paroxysm of pleasure that seemed to hit with the force of a thousand volts.

The legend of the ancient Persians believed that Oysters rose to the surface of the Sea on clear nights and were fertilised by drops of dew that turned into Pearls when they trapped the rays of the moon. I have had difficult periods in the past, but I have always weathered them, but the sore is still raw to touch yet. All I want to know is how to create something perfect; beautiful and everlasting because it seems these days life is not worth living if you have to compromise. Is the beggar being a chooser?

I digested the story I've just heard that the emotions are too raw; too close to the surface and still too confused because they pushed me over the edge on purpose and the love flowing between us would have lit up the sky in a blackout as a result of my so-called golden child who was my class - learner, but to be an Artist, the soul and mind and heart must be free. She should not have been a kind of learner who would expect more than I am willing to give. Well! She has a dirty mind and knows best for herself. Unfortunately, I am not made of crystal, and I do not break.

Blame is good for us even when we do not deserve it. If we so accept it, God is not angry. Always keep a good conscience and through it save you not from many reproaches, yet it shall bring you to the light. Fools may come nearer to God where the desire of or understanding keep wise men distant. We are always hiding from something aren't we? Either from ourselves or from each other or more often from God. To believe without understanding is easier for the foolish than for the wise, just like being more of a sinner and less of a fool or vice versa because out of doubt, evil can bring good.

God does not think as we do because if He did, He would make mistakes like we do hence the good; the bad and the mixed are alike and always trying to hide themselves.

I therefore suggest that you play your game, and the hour is not yet over or let my head stand for yours. Do not make Prisoners, for he or she who puts others in Prison is him or herself a Prisoner thus Wolcott said: "Each care drives a nail in our coffin, no doubt but each merry laugh again drives it right out."

Therefore having lived thus far, the rest of my life's journey ought not to be impossible but just a little more effort is required because the destiny of this world is not fixed hence those who look only at the surface of things often fall into this error.

In this life I learned to cope with each moment as it was, not thinking about the minutes just gone or those about to come, just the immediate now. I had to run away if they tried to make me go anywhere, I did not want to go. I 'd keep on running away until they let me stay in my hometown. I did not want to go through the hell I did. I worked all the hours God sent and I do not think I ever stopped hurting, as some people are living a rotten life.

Once I am out of sight and was not at any risk anymore and dismissed me from their minds. It is their doing; it is being them by making people know it's them and getting it right and making them listen. They could talk the birds off the trees and tails donkeys, but they turn to forget that I am not made of sugar, I will not break up and disappear.

They expected me to run like a secluded cat in the opposite direction and thought I would play the game according to their rules. This helped me realise that once the panic had gone, I knew I could cope, and I am adamant on that score.

Let me pull the chair round and sit on it back to front so that I could rest my arms across the top as the words had dried in my mouth and refused to be spoken because I kept going round in circle as there is a great deal I get wrong but I do my best to make the least of those things and the best of the ones that do work.

CHAPTER 3

THE DESTINY OF THIS WORLD IS NOT FIXED

What is so real about telling someone you love him or her in one sentence and then in the next that you love him or her. You will not let him or her do the one thing he or she most want to do, what is real or valuable about that? It is like you are trying to own him or her, not loving him or her and that hurts like the devil.

Love knows all things. It knows sorrow and laughter; knows endurance and action; knows hunger and growth; knows adventure and reverence and it also knows pride and magnanimity. For this reason, love approaches omniscience. Love contentedly suffers hardship and works miracles therefore it approaches omnipotence. It is further said, love is effervescent as it saturates and fuses. Love embraces thus it is flexible and adaptable. In my understanding, love really is the final reality.

What is happening in Ebumnandini? What could I possibly say that would make people believe me? All I want is everything to be logical and clear and sane. I am trying to make sense out of this. I am dead serious, and I am dead right but there is nothing earth shattering to report so - far. So, it goes.

I did not want to relive the heart-breaking experience hence I was trying to keep the story quiet. Why did they become in the first place for dropping their little bombshell? Oh He! Small mindedness clung to the people like tar to a wooden spoon. I now know the unthinkable as it had taken me so much courage to be where I am in the first place. I could act crazy if I wanted to, but I felt lost; a little confused and very tired because I could not make sense of it and that bothered the hell out of me.

They were not just smart but cleverer as they are keeping tabs on me for a reason and apparently that reason would arrive. I felt no fear for them, only for the void my conviction would create. My terror was for the people. I wondered in all humility how I had failed God. How I had been so early defeated? Shooting pains engulfed my heart like knives piercing into my chest but they are going to an early grave with their precious secret and they are going straight to the kingdom of hell. I put it out of my mind now. Well! I tried to, anyway because years and months had passed but of course I could not forget.

They all tried to nail me down. Someone was reluctant to take any kind of stand but he or she knew that the story was going to come out one way or the other. Who was my mouthpiece pertaining all this nonsense? When the Newspapers came out behind my back, it was still as warm as a loaf of freshly baked bread. Hell! These Papers were hot.

On the 4th of August 2016 when I appeared for the first time in my life in front of the Parole Board in Kroonstad Correctional Centre, I asked myself: What did these important men and women think of me? They are not stupid, and they are paid to be sceptical. Thanks to my Almighty God because they gave me the 20th of September 2016 to be the date of my release. They even advised me to go to Bhudaza Clerk of the Court to fill in the forms that could help me to cancel the Criminal Record. They even asked me, what is it that I will do to retain my reputation as a Teacher, and I gave them the answer. They therefore put it on my hands to deal with SACE because they said they know nothing about how the Department of Education works. All these were their final words.

Believe me. I am my beloved's and my beloved aremine. She is safe with me; she is more precious to me than anything or anyone in the world and nobody shall ever hurt her hence I wrote this letter to her on the 20th of May 2016 while in the Slammer.

You may doubtless be wondering why you have not heard from me. I apologize for the lack of courtesy by knowing your kind thoughts for me. I waited till I had cheerful news to send. I have asked much of you; I shall always ask much of you. In return I will give you all I can; do all I can to make you happy. I will never fail you. Trust me and I shall be satisfied you are so lovely, so sweet, so perfect and all mine.

I love you with all my heart and soul. You are my desire and delight. I love you even though I have nothing else to give but I will still give you love because my feelings are my own and could not be altered from outside.
O! Western wind, when will you blow? That the small rain down can rain; that my love is in my arms and I in my bed again. Love is the sweetest way, what else on earth can bring? I have had my eyes on you a long,

long time and I have sighed a sigh for you. You know I would die for you I do not know why I do?

I am spiritually with you all my life, I'll be so glad to be with you again See how cheerful I will greet you ; soothe you ; cheer you ; love you ; tease you ; flung away your cares and troubles . All life's worries are but bubbles and there is no sense in looking blue.

Taste deeply of the truth as it is in Jesus. There came the invasion of the radical lefts with their materialistic interpretation of the Universe and of life. Their non-idealistic and anti-religion programme and their appeal to class strife and force which marched with golden boots. I refuse to see red, refused to resort to force and now the guns are turned on me from my own camp.

In this country - Ebumnandini if not the whole world, there is nothing as absurd as ownership. Ownership is like a shell and the only one who profits by it, is the one who shuts him or herself up within it. To the one who desires to reach upward and grow, it is only a hindrance, for the shell exists only for the spineless animals. Ownership is always advocated by the spineless species.

The human heart must be re-sculptured because man - made morality has created the present avaricious economic system and degenerate politics. Christ alone can make all things new. The spirit of Christ - the Carpenter must be the Soul and creative dynamic of all real social reconstruction.

The Christian labourer should purify his or her motives, desires, and life. To discriminate against no one and to love all men with sincerity; to support each other not with selfish or aggressive motives and to lead one another toward altruistic as against materialistic goals. He or She must not be absorbed in his or her group to forget Society as a whole.

The labourer must recognize the transitory period through which the world is at present and acknowledge that, there are Politicians; Principals; Managers; Government Officials ...who are sincerely seeking for light and ready to do what is right. If his or her Employer like mine, be an Exploiter or Bossy. He or She should strive to show him or her the error of his or her ways by not resorting to violent measures.

It came to my realisation that Ebumnandini Employers are destroying people's lives; careers; reputations by retrenching; dismissing; suspending ...Employees unfairly. Justice on the other side are arresting; convicting, imprisoning ... people without concrete evidences by using flimsy circumstantial evidences, by also accepting bribes; by being bias hence corruption is too high instead of invention and creation. I therefore suggest that we as countrymen should intelligently, accurately swing our hammers and watch the results.

The labourer must have no mean opinion of himself. Away with self-depreciation! Be conscious of your worth as a labourer and glory in your role because the procedure's course is in creation. Do not get excited! A waste of nerve energy will get you nowhere - Be calm! Be steady! Let them do their worst. There is but one course for the labourers and that is production motivated by love. My research led me to the conviction that poverty had its roots in the situation.

I agree, unions are necessary but labour problems can only be solved by the inner awakening of the labourer. The labour movement and any social movement must first and foremost be moral and sacrificial. It must also treat the rich and the poor alike.

An employer should learn to treat their employees as human beings with respect and dignity. The employee shares the employer's family life; both should eat at the same table and work in the same room. They should join minds and hands in the same task; face each other as man to man; know each other and to understand each other.

The strange relationship between employer and employee in Ebumnandini has changed in such a way that the rights are all on the side of the employer and the employee has no choice or voice as to work but he or she should work ; the hour he or she should work and the wage or salary he or she should receive . In many cases working conditions are a scandal because hours are long, and wages or salaries are low.

In truth he or she who forgets the unemployed forgets God because God dwells among the lowliest of men; God sits on the dust - heap among the convicts; God stands at the door with the juvenile delinquents begging bread; God is among the sick. God stands in line with the unemployed in front of the employment agencies or bureaus. God visits the Prison cell before going to the Temple and He throngs with the beggars at the place of the rich.

No matter how long and loud we shout "Amen". Our empty stomachs are not filled. Where is the gate to His heaven of Amens where real salvation is to be found? In the presence of truth, steel chains and prison bars melt away. In the presence of truth, persecution and oppression are powerless. HO - HO! Fear the truth! To those who know God, pain is the supremist art.

I always say to my Soul, Let hurricanes roar! Let earthquakes rock and rend! Let typhoons unite their forces and rage! Let avalanches come!

Desperate people result to desperate measures for instance if a noose is continuously tightened about their necks until they expire. That will result to old scars to start surfacing and that for them it would be like going from one boiling pot into another hence they will go in and out prisons like walking through a revolving door.

The Public Protector must then be informed and involved as his or her duty is to investigate abuse of power; undue delay of appeals; court cases; causes of unemployment ...because people have to eat and they would pay and do anything to meet their needs as the prices of basic needs on the other hand are continuing skyrocketing and that is always causing stormy sessions in our parliaments.

I fear none of them because for me pain is the highest of arts. Those who are born of God must be as strong because without a price, God permits us to witness many earthly tragedies. To those who live intensely pain is a puzzle test and so to enrich the stuff of our lives, God has sown the earth with the seed of tears.

Look at the sky, look at the sun. Let your tears evaporate and then we will laugh. If God clothe the grass of the field which today is and tomorrow is cast into oven, shall He not much more clothe us. O! We of little faith.

The civilisation of steel and concrete separates mankind from the soil and the soil is God's footstool. The scent of the soil heals me hence I have no desire to become civilised and I want to live close to the soil. We will have to have hand to hand fight with nature in His effort to sustain life.

I discovered that Christianity is a religion of love and a Theological seminary is a school of love. A School of love should guide a mistaken student as God never abandons anyone. Before a Christian goes to church, let him or her visit the hospital; before he reads his or her Bible, let him or her help the beggar standing at his or her door. If he or she visits the Prison after going to the temple, does he or she not by so much delay his or her meeting with God?

CHAPTER 4

A SOLDIER OF MOVEMENT WHO AWAKENS THE CONSCIENCE

Religion is the greatest of all the arts. Alone is an art which takes in the whole of living and is an art of life itself. When we live by religion, we are able for the first time to sit before God's mirror. Even when I weep, shrouded in darkness of being falsely imprisoned and unfairly dismissed from work, God does not fail to see because my melancholy will one day melt away like a mist before the rising sun.

I had to beat back the blow with love and not with hate and to put my reliance on the justice of my cause and in soul force. I am eager to learn from the experience and experiments of others who had wrought effectively in this field from whom their precious souls were stolen.

The present evil order has stolen those whom I dearly loved and is killing us alive by putting even the innocent behind bars thereafter punishing us with Criminal Records which curb us from getting employment. Didn't the so-called "Offenders" punished enough? Didn't they get their punishments? If so, why still a grudge against them? Who is supposed to ask for forgiveness between the so-called "Offender even Innocent like me" and the so-called 'victim'? Why vice versa about this Victim's report issue because I believe that forgiveness is something a person do for him or herself and not everyone else because I believe a change must come from within.

It is like putting an oar into a stormy Sea. Every gain is followed by a backward swing. I determine that the liberation of all Ebumnandinans including the labourers and Offenders especially those who were falsely convicted with no relevant proof or concrete evidence, that for me is the only way to save the Ebumnandinans.

The ferment of social unrest and discontent had long been at work. The rumbling of a coming storm could be clearly heard in their ranks because they had to double check Offender's cases and convictions and bring back those who were wrongfully arrested and falsely convicted.

I have friends and followers by the hundreds scattered through every walk of life. The Government Officials and Police can harass me in my work, but they cannot with impurity play fast and loose with my personal freedom. No matter how elegant their beauty may be, it is after all parasitic beauty for which the boy or man went wrong, and the girl or woman led astray.

Confinement in the Nick for three or more years would be no hardship for me because God does not cast me off. Being the discipline of non-resistance and forgive and forget as my peaceful methods were employed under my leadership because we planned and directed our campaigns as a team and I took their demands to the authorities or in person pleaded their cause. The Prison Warders manifested all the leniency possible and treated me kindly and the fellow inmates also treated me with respect due to the fact of my work there as their Teacher and what I also did for them.

The Labour movement with which I related myself do not demand large possessions. They have but three demands - a chance to live; a chance to work and a chance to show the marks of a man.

I therefore have no desire to participate in Labour movements motivated by greed, where budgets can no longer be balanced hence so many strikes for instance Old age strikes; Students strikes; Service delivery strikes; Labour strikes ... Politicians becoming fat cats instead of helping people who voted for them hence the minky - mouse and stormy sessions in parliaments but the Procurers are still recruiting their victims from this ignorant, destitute class.

My friends and followers were alarmed at my rashes because I declared that I would find my greatest satisfaction in dying in action because in the Ebumnandini world of labour, the Labourers and unemployed are no longer free men. They are bound down by an economic and social order which made them slaves of circumstance and economic determinism. Poverty and exploitation wherever found are two of man's chief foes, degrading and destroying monsters. They play havoc with the finer human values and devastate Society.

I have to stand what the surge and flood of life runs strong because I am the man of the hour. I had lived with them. I had suffered with them. I had wept with them and I know them better than they know themselves. Their cause is my cause and their battles army. If COETU is the father of the labour movement in our country, I am the mother because my heart ; my Soul ; my sympathy and my understanding of the Employees as well as Innocents is like that of a mother - a wise mother because I oppose the use of violence and destructive tactics.

In building of a finer and fairer social order, I believe in Evolutionary rather than Revolutionary processes. I believe social reconstruction must be brought about through change. I believe in organisation rather than through violence and destruction because Revolution brought about through force is accompanied by tragic economic, moral and spiritual losses.

I wouldn't be silenced by Government's corrupt Departments as for instance the Departments of Education and Justice who were determined to take strong measures against me as they have already done by destroying my life ; reputation ; family and career but I am having my own ideas and ideals . I am militant in my defence as long as this disease still had me in its grip and death still stalked me.

I am a lone voice in the wilderness. I beat myself against an immovable wall as the Offenders had always existed and always would. False decrees that the fitter shall survive and the beaten sink to the bottom. If the conscience is educated, politics; economics; education and science will take care of themselves.

Like "Kagawa" I am a soldier of movement to awaken the conscience and he or she who hears the outcry of my conscience is my true friend because God's abode is in the conscience. When I help the Government, the

Government's Officials greet me with a smile but when I turn to assist my first and undying love for the poor, lost souls and disadvantaged, the Government Officials begin to darken their traits hence they put me behind bars to soft - pedal but all their doings will never stop me from my plans and goal because I never turn a deaf ear to a call of distress of our Government facing a financial famine. OH! Ebumnandini is in distress.

Unemployment in Ebumnandini is growing by leaps and bounds due to unfair dismissals, wrongful arrests and convictions, criminal records, corruptions ... Both the unemployed and the poor are sleeping out in the open, beaten by the winter winds and drenched by the chilling rain or the snow.

I hate things which only cause trouble. There is nothing more exhilarating than to walk unencumbered. If possessions abound. There is a haunting fear that they may be stolen. If you are beautifully dressed, you worry lest your clothes be soiled. If you are occupying the high rank, you are anxious that you will be thrown down and if you pride yourself on being erudite, you are cut to the quick if someone makes light of you. Strip you to the skin that is the way to walk these days.

Kagawa once said: “If we put aside and allow the life of the Universe to whisper to our hearts, living becomes pure joy. Then the heart will be detached from illusions and worldly cares would be overcome. Even amid the most chaotic scenes, there will be a stillness of soul which is undisturbedly.”

God’s Declaration: “The whole creation is mine. My life penetrates to the heart of every created thing. In the kitchen, it is one with the spirit of the fire. I am emerged into everything. I can dwell with the soot in the chimneys and find peaceful place with the flea under matted straw.”

When set free, I fly upward to the constellation of the Great Bear. I speed from star to star. I conceal myself in the depths of my loved one's dressing mirror. If I love the whole creation, I can travel about it with the utmost freedom.

A fool makes many by contact and example; by word and by deed; also, by gesture and by appearances so that wherever he or she goes, foolishness goes with him or her. By being a fool, you upset others so that they also become fools in their uprisings and their up settings therefore, it was them made fools of people because they upset everything.

People are so foolish, yet so full of wisdom. They have made mock of me; they have made a fool of me; they have told lies of me, yet I am not angry with them but grateful. Learn of me. Maybe what I am talking about is too big a bite for their wits and maybe I was not fit to lick their boots because they are those who have a little and I am one of those who have nothing.

Nothing that goes into people's ears find lodging in their heads and their mouths are for noise only, never has it been heard utter sense. Their brains are the brains of a beast and one must break them before one can get at them. People talk of guardian Angels as if they are great things; bright; shining and beautiful outside of ourselves, but I think, maybe they are little dark things, moving about in our insides like fleas.

Our conscience is like a flea because it always sees a man naked. When it gets to the weakest part of him or her, it bites and there is no running away from it. A flea may only jump a pig's length while the man is on run for twenty kilometres or more, but it is still on him or her even when he or she stops running. The man may get to the other side of him or herself or of the world; He or she may even turn him or herself inside out or upside down but he or she has not got rid of the flea yet.

I could put my hope in anything I want, but to put it in hope itself, is just pure foolishness because whenever a subordinate like myself shows any extra - ordinary capacity and consequently attains to a position of influence, his or her Master is apt to regard him or her with jealousy and fear thereafter often destroy him or her ruthlessly on the first shadow of a pretext.

It goes without saying that a negativism which answers safety is far greater blessing than a positivism which leads to ruin hence the parasitic life makes its appearance in ever - changing forms for instance: Those who are a little clever consider the parasitic life their right . Therefore, a sin is that had fallen away from life, from the absolute and from the eternal.

God must not be thought of as an abstract somebody or a thing because God is life Himself hence life generates life. The man is the receiver of life and the giver of life itself hence life surges in upon me and moves eternally.

Life is a miracle ; death is a miracle ; law is a miracle ; reality is a miracle ; illness is a miracle ; recovery is a miracle ... and everything has an existence independent of mine for instance , the transformation of the caterpillar is a miracle ; ants wriggling in the sand is a miracle and so on and on .

God as life fills both the inner and the outer of all His Creatures. He is the Creator of all Creatures; the Creator of absolute values; the Preserver and Unfolder of all things and He is the only One who will be able to cease going astray. Life because of its reality is absolute thus life in me has an end in view and it is personalized.

CHAPTER 5

FORGIVE AND FORGET NOT REVENGE AND REGRET

God is neither objective nor subjective but life absolute. Life as to Him all things are holy. I as God's fool for evermore I will walk along the straight line which connects God and myself because he or she who loves not, knows no God, for God is love.

I pray because I am living being and because I was made to grow. A growing being has certain requirements and for that I place the requirements before the Lord of life. I pray to God regarding everything and I do not pray simply for myself because where love exists, there must be salvation. In the past here in Ebumnandini was no evil potent for evil but we have tasted it and it was bitter but today it is worse.

I have decided to write this message to everyone about the master who has never given up on anyone of us. Therefore, faith means realisation of the fact that one is loved. The belief that love is stronger than disease, stronger than disaster and stronger than death. When we live by religion, we are able for the first time to sit before God's mirror. Religion may be looked upon as a means in the economy of life by which one learn first to suffer loss in order to get great gain hence the grain of wheat fall into the ground and die abides itself alone but if it dies, it bears most fruits.

The religion which exploits people uses the greatest number of words just like a Capitalist who squeezes millions out of the working class and considers theft of one flower vase an irreparable loss hence the rich cannot understand the hardships of the toiling poor.

For that reason, it is most dangerous to make oneself the centre in judging the total situation.

If only God lives, I am content to die because death to me is the pathway to Him. Even now it is He who gives me life. If life is God's gift, is death not one of the variations of life also the work of His hand?

We must not build boundaries in the world of the soul because the soul is an internationalist. The machine was invented by God using human brains as a blessing for mankind.

I would like to convert all the prisons of today into hospitals because the so-called criminals or offenders whom I have known are most of them sick people. Not only are they the prey of either physical or mental disease but they also grew up in a diseased Society because some of them are under - nourished, some unemployed, some have criminal records ...

Society itself has a criminal tendency which is self-caused lunatic, for instance the liquor bottle stores, the Tobacco shops, the prostitute's quarters; the army, the newspapers... Don't all of them show symptoms of a diseased mentality? I believe God and His cure alone can heal it.

When suffering envisions, a great goal is transformed into privilege. It is therefore necessary to ignore pain and look at the totality of one's mission in life as the Martyr chooses pain as pathway to glory. Whenever there is an absence of beauty, there is a hidden sense of shame therefore nothing is so curious as courtesy. Why do we shake hands? Why do we bow?

The man that laughs is a Doctor without a Diploma because the merrier the laugh, the longer the life. A good, honest, and hearty laugh is said to be the best of all medicines for the mind and the best of all medicines for the body, one of the greatest blessings that man can enjoy is a good laugh. It clearly stated that, beyond the grave, we shall have more joy more fun and more laughter than sorrow.

In my research I discovered and learnt that: Laugh yourself heartily and you will feel better. Make your friend laugh and you will make him or her happier but make your enemy laugh and he or she will hate you less. Make a stranger laugh and you will give him or her more confidence and make a sorrowful laugh and you will lessen their grief. Make the desponding laugh and you will raise their hopes. It is further said, make the old laugh and you will make them feel younger and make the child laugh and you will make him or her better tempered, healthier, more happy, and more loving. Hence, I am always saying, books bring more joy and do better than mortal tongue can tell.

Laughter is said to be an external expression of joy as it is the most salutary expression of all the bodily movements. It also agitates both the body and soul at the same time hence it promotes digestion, circulation and perspiration thus enlivens the power in every human organ in his or her body hence I love it when the child laughs with rippling and gentle which is so wild and so free and that is the merriest sound in the world for me.

According to Henry Ward Beecher, mirth on the other hand is the sweetest wine of human life and Dr Fuller said, harmless mirth is the best cordial. In my study I learnt that Mirth is the medicine of life because it cures ills and calms its strife. It softly smooths the brow of care and writes a thousand graces there.

It was a good job. Best I ever had. I am sorry, it did not last as I have planned from which I made good money too. At first Principals of Schools treated me swell from the time I met them but on the arrival of the little yellow devil in my work who evidently does not care of what she and her little army has done and said about me and my family as they wanted me to kneel at their feet with my arms around their knees for something I did not do or the crime I did not commit. They know that too. Deep down in their hearts, they know my innocence.

Today I have no more job than snakes got hips just because I was paid by the Government, the new so-called "Employer" always thought he owns me. Well because I laughed with them, they thought I am like them. My so-called "Employer" used to say: "You are working for me, nobody else. Keep your mouth shut about what goes on here and I'll look after you."

He was always talking about sex appeal and loving as if he knew more stories than any man, I ever talked to. He had always thought he was a great lover and that women liked him for something else besides his money. Nobody ever told him that he was not so hot.

I discovered that the mother of the so-called "Victim" knew where her bread was buttered because my so-called "Employer - Boss" is just as white inside as he is black out hence she had him standing on his ears because I believe she is the type of a woman who kids rich folks along and depends on them for living and makes them think she likes it.

She really puts the bee on him as she has a talent to hook new butter - and - egg men with bucks so that they could buy her everything she wants and squeezing them and later tell them that they should not think they are buying her heart. I also discovered that most of her victims become so high with drinks and didn't know "B" from Bottle of Whisky and take out women's pictures and bent them and stamp on them, then make love to them and tear them up.

I believe a yellow woman sure did drive him crazy hence I was unfairly dismissed from work; wrongfully arrested and wrongfully imprisoned using flimsy so-called circumstantial evidence, using hearsay witnesses, why were the Detectives and police who handled my case were not questioned? On the day of my conviction where was my lawyer who knows about my case and where was the Prosecutor who handled the case and knows more about my so-called case? Why sudden substitutes who knew nothing about my case? Why so much inconsistency on my so-called charges and what is my actual charge? I am still having many unanswered questions based on my so-called case. Where is the truth and fairness in my conviction and dismissal from both Departments? What about the procedure?

Now or Never because the bridge has been built by both Labour and Justice Departments, for that we should meet one another halfway across the bridge. Just because I am strong enough to handle pain, does not mean I deserve it. Well I am not perfect I do make mistakes and sometimes I hurt people but when I say

"Sorry" I actually mean it but bear in mind that I was born without them so guess what? I can live without them.

We only live once but if we do it right, once is enough hence worry for me is a total waste of time because it doesn't change anything but all it does is steal our joy and keeps us very busy doing nothing. Every time when I feel a little down, there would be another time when I would be able to laugh again hence for me some times , Silence is a really good answer thus I forgive and forget not revenge and regret. I never give up but go over; go under; go around or go through but never give up.

Before I get drunk, before my pen jams and before I dance to the song of the year and lose my paperwork, I wish you to read; understand and decide hence I always pray:

Lord, I come before you to praise Your Name and glorify You Father. Cancel every curse and negative word that ever been spoken over me; my life; my family and my future in the Name of Jesus Christ.

I discovered that, the audience that storms the box Office of the Theatre to gain entrances to a sensational show is small and sleepy compared with the throng that crashes the Court - House door when something concerning real life and death is to be laid bare to the public.

I became aware for the first time in my life that the Courtroom is full of starving men and women shut within closed doors; guarded by Police wearing uniforms to confound the simple inside the sacred precinct and this dispels all hope of mercy to the unlettered; the poor and helpless who scarcely dare express themselves above a whisper in any such forbidden place.

What I experienced has made me realise that the Stage ; the Arena and the Courts are alike in that each has its audience; thirsting to drink deeply of the passing show and those playing the parts vie to success and use whatever skill and talent they possess.

An Actor may fumble his or her lines, but a Lawyer needs to be letter - perfect and at least he has to use his or her wits. He or She may forget him or herself and often does but never for a moment can he or she lose sight of his or her client who was me at that moment. No wonder that ambitious; imaginative youths crowd the profession of law because there they feel that they themselves will find the opportunity to play a real part in the Comedies as well as Tragedies of life.

Everyone no matter how small his or her chances may be, tries to hold the centre of some Stage where the multitude will scan his or her every move. To most lads it seems as though the Courts were organised to furnish them a chance to bask in the public eye, for in this field the adventure of life will never fail but prove interesting; exciting and changeful to the end. Not only he or she have the destinies of men to protect and preserve but his or her own standing and success to create.

Chancery cases are not interesting or exciting however these are supposed to be heard by a Magistrate or Judge or Jurors who listens long enough to feel satisfied that the case promises to consume considerably time and work and interfere with many hours of leisure thereafter he or she refers it to a Master in Chancery who is a lawyer friend of his or her own appointment and who is paid by fees that come directly from the Litigants.

CHAPTER 6

NO JUSTICE EITHER IN OR OUT OF COURTS

The master in Chancery employed a court reporter who takes the evidence in shorthand while he or she takes a nap in an adjoining office. After the client's resources are exhausted by the court, the documents are locked up in a safe to await the blowing of Gabriel's horn.

If it is a real case for instance criminal or civil, it is usually tried by a prosecutor with an assistance and direction of the magistrate or judge or juror and in that every moment counts. Neither the lawyers nor audience nor even the court goes to sleep. In such cases, it is not the law alone or the facts that determine the result, but it is always the element of luck and chance which looms large.

The litigants and their lawyers are supposed to want justice, but there is no such thing as "justice" either in or out of Court. In fact, Justice cannot be defined due to the lack of proof. We assume that the word "justice" has a meaning and that the common idea of the definition is correct without even seeking to find out what is the common meaning.

How do people reach Justice through the courts? In my understanding, the lawyer's idea of justice is a verdict for his or her client and really is the sole end for his or her aims. It goes without saying that lawyers always do their best to get men on the magistrate or judge or juror who are apt to decide in favour of their clients. I then realised that it is not the experience of magistrate or judge or juror, neither is their brain power that is the potent influence in their decisions.

I learnt that , In spite of the power that the Courts exercise over the verdict of the Magistrate or Judge or

Juror , still the finding of the Prosecutors is very important and sometimes conclusive but a skilful Lawyer does not tire him or herself hunting for learning or intelligence in the box because if he or she knows much about man and his or her making ; that all beings act from emotions and instincts and that reason is not a motive factor because if deliberation counts for anything then it is to retard decision .

My experienced has made me realise that, the nature of the man either him or herself is the element that determines the Magistrate's bias for or against his or her fellow men. Assuming that a Magistrate is not a halfwit, his or her intellect can always furnish good reasons for following his or her instincts and emotions.

There is no doubt that, most Magistrate's trials are contests between the rich and the poor for instance , if the case concerns money , it is apt to be a case of damages ; for injuries of some sort claimed to have been inflicted by someone . Such cases are usually defended by Insurance Companies or Banks or Factories.

If a Criminal case like so-called mine, it is practically always the poor who are on trial and for that reason, the most important point to learn is whether the prospective Magistrate is humane. This must be discovered in devious ways because as soon as the Court sees what the Lawyer wants, they block the game as it happened in my so-called “Case”. What next then?

I realised that, the Magistrate is watching not only the evidence but the attitude of each Lawyer and the parties involved in all their moves and every step is fraught with doubt if not mystery hence choosing Magistrates is always a delicate task. The more a Lawyer knows of life; human nature; psychology and the reactions of the human emotions, the better he is equipped for the subtle selection of the Magistrate which is good and true in this undertaking.

In my research I also discovered that, everything pertaining to the prospective Magistrate needs to be questioned and weighed; his or her nationality; business; religion; politics; family; social standing; friends; habits; the books and Newspapers he or she likes and read. Involved in it all is the Magistrate's method of speech; the kind of clothes he or she wears and above all his or her associates; residence and origin.

Selecting a Magistrate is of the utmost importance hence the Lawyer should know both sides of the case. If the client is a Landlord or a Banker, then the Magistrate who is sympathetic to that class will be wanted in the box. A man who looks neat; trim and smug will be sure to guard your interests as he or she would his or her own because his or her entire environment has taught him or her that all values are measured in cash and he or she knows no other worth. I discovered that, every Lawyer seeks for a Magistrate of the same sort of man as his or her client; a man who will be able to imagine him or herself in the same situation and realise what verdict the client wants of which never happened in my so-called "Case".

In my research I also learnt that , Lawyers are just as carefully concerned about the likes and dislikes ; the opinion and fads of Magistrates or Judges or Jurors hence every Lawyer who represents the poor avoids a trial by the Court because all property rights are much safer in the hands of Courts than of Magistrates or Judges or Jurors .

To the ordinary Observer a man is just a man but to the Student of life and Human Beings, every pose and movement is a part of the personality for instance, a man may seem to be a certain mould but a wife or a friend or an enemy entering into his or her life may change his or her most vital views; desires and attitudes so that he or she will hardly recognize him or herself as the man he or she once seemed to be.

It is therefore obvious that, if a Litigant discovers one of his or her friends in the Jury panel, he or she could make a close guess to how certain facts surrounding circumstances and suppositions would affect his or her mind and actions.

It is said, a Magistrate or Judge or Juror who laughs, hates to find anyone guilty as Shakespeare once said: "Yonder Cassius has a lean and hungry look, he thinks too much, such men are dangerous." Therefore I suggest that, Lawyers should never take a wealthy man as a Magistrate or Judge or Jury because he or she will convict even the innocent like myself, unless the defendant is accused of violating the anti - trust law or selling worthless stock.

I discovered that, a good defensive Lawyer wants imaginative Magistrate or Judge or Juror and is not interested in his or her morals. If a man is instinctively kind and sympathetic, take him or her. Assuming that the Lawyer represents one of the underdogs because of injuries received or because of indictment brought forth by the Prosecutor who refer to him or herself as the "State", what sort of man will you seek as the Magistrate or Judge or Juror?

A Lawyer should be aware that the Magistrate or Judge even the Juror is emotional ; kind and sympathetic but if his or her feelings go deeper than that, he or she will be found guilty of malpractice if he or she gets rid of him or her except for the strongest reasons.

Lawyers should bear in mind that an Afrikaans Speaking or Englishman is not as good as a Blackman but still he or she has come through a long tradition of individual rights and is not afraid to stand alone. In fact, he or she is never sure that he or she is right unless the great majority is against him or her. An Afrikaans Speaking Magistrate like the one who falsely convicted me is not keen about individual rights except where they concern his own way of life because for him, Liberty is not a theory but it is the way of living. Well! He still wants to do what is right and he is not afraid.

In my research I discovered that, if the Magistrate or Judge or Juror is a Catholic, then he or she loves music and art. For that he or she must be emotional and he or she will want to help you and so give him or her a chance.

Christians on the other hand are too serious and solemn people who seem to think that pleasure is wicked and that only gloomy and dyspeptic can be trusted to convict.

The Baptists are more hopeless than the Presbyterians. They too are apt to think that the real home of all outsiders is hell. As a Lawyer, you will not want them on the Jury or to be Magistrate or Judge therefore the sooner they leave the better. *Wo Hhe*! Worst! If he or she is a Presbyterian and enters the Jury or becomes a Magistrate or Judge in your case and carefully rolls up his or her Umbrella and calmly and critically sits down.

Let him or her go because he or she is cold as the grave; he or she knows right from wrong although he or she seldom finds anything right. He or She believes in his or her religion and eternal punishment. It is said, get rid of him or her with the fewest possible words before he or she contaminates the others unless you and your client are Presbyterians too. It is clearly indicated that Presbyterians are a bad lot because even though you may be a Presbyterian, your client most likely is guilty.

The Methodist are worth considering because they are nearer the Soil. Their religious emotions can be transmitted into love and charity. They are not half bad even though they will not take a drink. It is said, if chance sets you down between a Methodist and the Baptist, you will have to move towards the Methodist to keep warm.

The Lutherans are almost sure to convict and for that reason plead your client guilty and go down the docket because he or she learns about sinning and punishing from the Preacher and dares not doubt and quote: "A person who disobeys must be sent to hell." Is it what happened to me in my so-called "Case?" because such Magistrate refers to themselves as having a God's word for that.

It is further said, it is best to a Universal or Unitarian with some care, for they may be Prohibitionists but do not accept a Prohibitionist because he or she is too solemn, holy, and dyspeptic. He or She knows your client would not have been indicted unless he or she were a drinking person and anyone who drinks is guilty of something, probably much worse than he or she is charged with although it is not set out in the indictment.

Neither would he or she have employed you as a Lawyer, had he or she not been guilty. Is it what happened when I was sentenced for imprisonment for the crime I did not commit just because I am drinking?

I discovered that among the twelve men in a Jury Box or if none - the Magistrates or Judges or Jurors are all degrees of alertness: all sorts of ideas and a variety of emotions. Lawyers too are to them important factors in the outcome because Lawyers and Prosecutors are closely observed by the Magistrate or Judge or Juror. They are liked or disliked because of what they say, how they speak or pronounce their words or part their hair.

It may be that a Lawyer is disliked because he or she talks too little or too much, more often "Too much". A Lawyer of subtlety should know when to stop and when to go on and how far to go. As a rule, he or she must not seem to be above the Magistrate or Judge or Juror nor below him or her. He or She must not strive for effect because he or she often meets baffling situations not easily explained.

Sometimes it is better for him or her to talk of something else and his or her explanations must not be too fantastic or ridiculous. It does not harm to admit the difficulty of the situation; to acknowledge that the circumstance or that seems against him or her because many facts in Courts point to guilt but in another light these facts may appear harmless. Lawyers therefore are apt to interpret deeds and motives as they wish them to appear.

CHAPTER 7

A NEW BROOM SWEEPS CLEAN

I learnt that; most actions are subject to various inferences. Sometimes quite improbable but none the less true. Identifications show common example of mistakes hence many men and women are in Prison and some are sent to death through mistaken Identifications. How many times have you met some person whom you believed to be an old - time friend and have found yourself greeting a total Stranger mainly in Public places like Restaurants?

Many Identifications in courts are made from having seen a person but once and under conditions not critical. Many are made from descriptions and photographs urged on by detectives, lawyers and others who are vitally interested in the results. From all this, it is easy to see that many people are convicted being guiltless of crime.

In situation of strong agitation, acquittals are rare, and sentences made long and barbarous and inhuman. The magistrate, judge or juror is as unconcerned about the actual meaning of it all just like the soughing wind rustling the leaves of a tree just outside the Court - house door.

I discovered that, women magistrates take their new privilege seriously. They are all puffed up with the importance of the part and they feel they play and are sure they represent a great step forward to the world. They believe sex is co - operating in a great cause. Well! Like the rest of male lawyers, women lawyers do not know which way is forward and which is backward or whether either one is any way at all.

The magistrate, judge or juror is an important part of the machinery and administration of the Court and they are not lacking knowledge of the law. The ordinary rules for the administration of the law are rather simpler and not difficult to follow hence they should be students of life even more than the law.

I discovered that, lawyers and carpenters, bricklayers and saloon keepers, teachers and politicians are not alike. No two have the same Education or fitness and natural understanding of themselves therefore Biology and Psychology which form the basis of understanding human conduct should be considered.

When the magistrate, judge or juror is a good or bad one depends on the point of view. They are like the rest of us because now and then, some outstanding figures will roll up their sleeves as it were and vigorously set to work to reform the Courts and get an efficient administration of justice.

This will be seconded by the Newspapers by lashing Courts for the Magistrates or Judges or Juror's past;

present and prospective into spasm of virtue that brings down the Innocents like myself and guilty together by always assuming that there are guilty and innocent. For a time, every defendant is convicted and soon the campaign reaches the Courts, after ruining a few lives and reputations, then the frenzy is over and life goes on smoothly and tranquillity as before. One big word that stands over Courts and other human activities is "Futility."

The Courts may be unavailing; Lawyers stupid and both as dry as dust, but the combination makes for something interesting and exciting which opens avenues that seem to lad somewhere of which are liberty; lives and fortunes are often at stake. Appeals for assistance and mercy rend the air for those who care to hear.

In all questions we are frequently influenced by some statements which were spoken at the eventful time which determines fate and the most unforeseen.

Accidental meetings sometimes result in seemingly new and strange fateful family lines. In fact, all that occurs in life is an endless sequence of events resulting from the wildest chance as a result. I can think of nothing, not even war that has brought so much misery to humans hence for me Prisons and all of it is so futile.

A new broom sweeps clean as it leaves no speck on the floor; under the bed or in the darkest corners of life but the new Magistrates or Judges or Jurors believe that the welfare of the State depends on the verdict which makes a vast difference to the unfortunates like myself, facing cruel and narrow - minded Magistrates or Judges or Jurors who pass judgement on the fellow man and to the defendants which might mean the fate of life rather than death.

Life for me, depends on the automatic taking in and letting out of breath, but in no way is it lengthened or made happier by deep thinking or wise acting. What is one life more or less in the general spawning? It may float away on the tide or drop to the depth of Oblivion; broken; crushed and dead. The great Sea is full of embryo with lives ready to take the places of those who have gone before.

One more unfortunate life dies as the endless stream flaws on and little it matters to the wise Magistrate or Judge or Juror who coldly pronounce long string of words in droning cadence and the victims are removed hence they come and go but the Magistrate or Judge or Juror keeps on chanting senseless phrases laden with doom upon the bowed heads of those before them.

No Scientific attitude towards crime can be adopted until Lawyers like Physicians and Scientists recognize that the cause and the effects determine the comfort of men. Now and then some learned Courts take a big view of life but scarcely do make an impression until some public brainstorm, drives them back in their treatment of crime to the methods of sorcery and conjury.

Many of the incurable victims of crimes are like those who were incurable victims of disease because they are products of vicious and incompetence soothsayers who control their destinies. Every human being whether Parents; Teachers like me; Physicians or Prosecutors should make the comfort and happiness of their dependants their first concern.

I believe the life of almost any unfortunate if rightly understood can be re-adjusted to some plan of order and system instead of being left to drift on to ruin; the victim of ignorance; hatred and chance.

I discovered that, if the Physician so completely ignored natural causes as the Lawyers and Magistrates or Judges or Jurors then the treatment of the disease would be relegated to witchcraft and magic and the dungeon thus the rack would once more hold high carnival in driving devils out of sick and afflicted. When Lawyers; Courts and Laymen accept the scientific theory which the Physicians forced upon the world long years ago, then men will examine each so-called delinquency until they discover its cause and then learn how to remove the cause. This requires sympathy; humanity; love of one's fellow man and a strong faith in the power of knowledge and experience to conquer the maladies of men.

These will lead to the forum of Lawyers possibly growing smaller and the Court - house may lose its spell, but the world will profit a millionfold by a kindlier and more understanding relation towards all humankind.

Without a fair knowledge of the mechanism of man, the motives and urges that govern his or her life will idle to venture to fathom a situation but with some knowledge. Officers and the Public can be most useful in preserving and protecting those who need such help. Even though I went through such unfortunate experience I will not give up as did Abraham Lincoln who was the sixteenth President of United State who lost six times but never gave up.

OH GOSH! Seeing the way in which this thing had come to pass, I said within myself , they had planned this all along as my so-called "Employer" is good in talking; manipulating and destroying other people's lives; families; careers and reputations . Such matters he knew well but of greater things he knows nothing, for he had never tasted his bitter medicine nor felt the pain in his entire life hence his letters must be obeyed and his commandments to be done.

I then realised that, truly for Holy obedience is to be silent hence I refrained my tongue from words and resolved to put my thoughts and words on paper. For I work not, neither can I preach. Seeing that I can do nothing either in labour or in Prayer and see my wife and my siblings upon their errands, one behind the other and I do naught but fill my belly with the food that they provide. I thought if they perceive this, certainly shall I be an evil case, for they will cast me out amongst the dogs and non will take pity on the glutton and the idle man.

I thought if I gave my Lawyers even more money than they asked or demanded, it would awaken their interests in my so-called "Case". When come, would cause them to talk eloquently regarding it. Surprisingly during the process, I was conscious of a queer uneasy feeling that something bad was going to happen in my life. I think almost all of us know how it is with the Cyclone at Sea, right in the centre we find a calm area while the hell is let lose all around.

I think it is time I get off my chest that without a good purse; a good cause; a good Lawyer; a good Counsel; a good evidence; a good Magistrate and a good luck, you are in real trouble with the Ebumnandini Law

under both Labour and Justice Departments hence the so-called Magistrates and Commissioners under labour sums up by saying:
"You have heard all the evidence as well as me; you have also heard what the learned Counsel have said. If you believe what the Counsel for the Plaintiff has told you, your verdict will be for Plaintiff, but if on the other hand, you believe what the Defendant's Counsel has told you, then you will give a verdict for the Defendant . But if you are like me and do not believe what either of them have said, then I'll be hanged if I know what you will do."

Shall I speak my thought? Shall I work my will? I will do that which I can. All Human Beings should know and hear and receive that God refuses none who seeks His face in love. It is not because some cannot see how a thing can be done and that therefore it cannot be done.

I discovered that, no human being has sufficient knowledge to lightly use the word "Impossible" because many useful; necessary and beautiful things will with no doubt be done and that will astonish the world.

It came to my realisation that , mankind may find a way of living healthy in the Tropics or of making Tropics into healthy Countries or regulating the rainfall by planting forests ; they may find modes of curing the supposed incurable diseases like HIV/AIDS ; Ebola ... ; They may get new motive powers out of water ;air and other sources to supersede steam as they have already done for instance "Electricity "

I have also realised that , Humanity is getting less vindictive and more just and kind for instance , let us consider the savage modes of execution that have been used as punishment of real or imaginary offences like burning people alive ; tearing limb from limb; death sentence ; crucifying ; throwing people to wild animals or beasts and so on . All these has ceased now throughout the world and humanity had dispense with more painless form of punishment for example, Murderers are currently humanly looked upon hence guillotine has been abolished and replaced by Maximum Prisons.

All human beings will be brothers and sisters and all of us would be friendly if we only had a proper introduction to each other and understand one another. I also realised that, all the great religions of the world are teaching unity of man and all great minds of the world have and are still teaching the unity of mankind hence for me the whole earth is the fatherland of the noble - minded .

CHAPTER 8

GREAT MINDS THINK ALIKE

Everywhere I look, I see evidence of the unity of mankind because everywhere humans are possessed of the same possessions which are, for instance, the same love and hate, the same hopes and fears and the same aspirations.

Education on the other hand, makes all the difference between the civilised people and the savage. In my opinion, if all people throughout the world can be taught to read in one common language and get plenty of good reading then mankind at large would become vastly better than they are currently and crime would diminish and friendliness would increase even ignorance would vanish.

I learnt that great minds think alike. People like Socrates, Nelson Mandela, Shakespeare, Mahatma Gandhi, Moses, Muhammad, Buddha, Plato, and others, they did not belong to one race. No mankind reads their writings can believe it due to the same thoughts and breathe through all, thereby show the unity of the human mind. Here lies the hope of the future and the potent agency to re-unite all races. In my research I also discovered that the evidence of the unity of the race is the ability of all nations to intermarry. For instance, marry a young healthy man to any healthy woman on the globe and they will have a family.

Mankind managed to beat all animals running on the land and swimming on the water and nearly managed to beat all birds flying through the air by using machine very light and very strong like the anatomy of the bird and the aeroplane for instance was invented.

All these would have been pronounced "Impossible" and yet mankind has done it all for instance human beings are able to send heavily - laden carriages for thousands of miles swifter than the fastest race horse by using huge ships many miles an hour against wind and tide ; they are able to illuminate with more than thousands lights in a moment by using electricity for instance lighting thousands and thousands of houses ; factories; shops and so on; They are able to cut off arms and legs without giving the patient the slightest pain and they able to do more and more.

It is said, all the thousands and thousands other wonderful things would have been pronounced "Impossible "hundreds and hundreds of years ago. Today people find other better modes of travel, they have more rapid and easy modes of intelligent communication between distant people and able to do thousands of things. Today the human being can invent means to bring the dangerous lightning with safety to the earth and he or she could invent means to go up miles into the air and return to the earth safely. People managed to invent machines to do the work of thousands of men and women and many other things.

In my research I discovered that the progress of the English speaking race throughout the British Empire and the United States during the past many years far exceeds that of any other people ever existed and has exceeded the total progress of all other nations in the world and currently the English speaking race governs nearly more than a half of the entire world.

It is said, the Anglo - Saxon is the least clannish of all the nationalities, but he feels at home in any country and amongst any people. This English-speaking race has produced “London “which is the largest; richest and mightiest City ever existed including “New York” with its more or less sixty others beautiful Cities. It is said, in Countries where the English Speaking race have settled , they have cleared forests ; made roads ;

bridges ; covered the Countries with modes of communication in every direction and started innumerable Industries beyond all precedent in the History of mankind .

It is also said, the English speaking race at present own more or less than half the Capital of the world; do plus - minus half banking of the world and produce more than half the literature and Inventors of the world.

India on the other hand has stopped bloodshed; abolished slavery and put down human sacrifice and is still doing the greatest work. South Africa on the other has successfully dealt away with Apartheid and fought for democracy; avoided civil war; abolished guillotine still trying to bring other changes.

The horrible curses of our History like slavery; human sacrifice; cannibalism and others have gradually diminished and progressive humanity feature like Hospitals; Refugee's camps and Charitable

Institutions of all kinds have increased tremendously throughout the civilised world. We see evidences that we are progressing from a cruel and unfeeling past into a more humane future.

War like all other evils is gradually diminishing and becoming more humane because the proportion of men killed in wars throughout the world in the olden days was very high because, powerful and fierce tribes would exterminate one or several tribes.

Our Ancestors lived upon wild fruits, wild animals, and wild herbs. They were naked or dressed in the skins of wild animals and they were constantly exposed to lions; bears and other wild and dangerous animals. They lived in all weathers under the trees on in dens and caves of the earth. Vast multitudes of them were doing behests of greater Tyrants and living in hovels badly clad and badly fed but today slavery is almost abolished.

The religion of our Ancestors with some mixture of truth in them were superstitious; degrading and cruel due to human sacrifices, bloody sacrifice of animals; putting poor helpless people to painful and shameful deaths due to witchcraft for believing in different faith.

Today every human being can hold that which he or she believes to be true without fear of State persecution and true religion does not suffer but is advancing. Goodness of all religions of mankind is more generally preached, believed in, and practiced than ever. We may rest assured that the religion will become more and more one of reason; simplicity and love instead of being one force; mystery ceremonies.

In the olden days, there have been the Government of Chieftains; popular men; Patriarchs; Priests; Nobles and Kings. Sometimes two or more of these forms were combined. It has been stated that, from the earliest Historic times up to the present three quarter of the rulers throughout the world have been Kings. E.W. Cole further stated that, there have been a few Republics which have been short-lived.

Political and Religious liberty is these days greater by means of the progress of medical; sanitary and surgical knowledge and for that, many diseases are prevented and cured. For me, religion which should be the blessing but has often been the greatest curse is surely going to become purified and more humane. Our Education system on the other hand has become freer and better.

Mankind have become more enlightened because the Republican form of Government or the Government by the people has become more established. In my point of view, this is the best and fairest form of Government that ever existed in every community because all human beings have an equal right to help to govern themselves and each other hence it is the most firm and lasting form of government.

The intellectual inequalities of mankind will cause the most gifted and most respected to manage public affairs while the mass of people like myself by their free votes will elect them to do so. These days mankind has gradually formed into large Governments and since the formation of these Governments, wars have become fewer as civilised welfare is far more humane than savage warfare.

Some people say war is necessary to keep down the population of the world. This idea for me is heartless and thoughtless because the world in my understanding is large enough and fruitful enough to support innumerable times its present population. Water: warmth and earth can produce vegetation anywhere and for that reason there need be no fear of starvation on the earth if mankind can only manage their resources properly.

It may be feared that the world is too large for one Supreme Government to manage but it is not so by any means because if we reflect upon the comforts and enjoyments of the present time as compared them with the past, we shall find that the difference is immensely in our favour .

In my research I discovered that the world is getting practically smaller every day because Education; Cell phones; Computers; Sports; Transport and Commerce are networking it in all directions. Travellers on the other hand are bringing the people nearer together and making them better acquainted with each other. Today we can send a message round the world in few hours because of these rapid means of communication which are extending and practically shortening distances everywhere.

I also discovered three of the great causes of crime which are Poverty, Drink and Ignorance. There is no doubt that Drink - Alcohol directly and indirectly is the cause of more than the half of the crime which is committed by directly exciting the passions and indirectly producing degradation of the person and poverty. The wrongs: bodily and mental tortures inflicted upon mankind by mankind are now less part cruel as they once were.

I learnt that, the Federation of the World does not mean that one country is to vexatiously interfere in the domestic concerns of another anymore, as it was when the Federal of British Government interfered in the domestic concerns of us Ebumnandinans; Canadians; Australians and New Zealanders hence the local self - government exists in every country.

Federal these days does not mean the enslaving of nations but the fraternal joining in a mutual agreement to abate the enormous cost and inhuman curse of war between nations; education; common currency and other things, for the common good and socialisation of all mankind. This kind of Federation will bring all mankind together in closer bonds of mutual self-respect, love and friendship.

I am happy to free people from mental slavery by saying , it is consummation to which everything seems to point as we have seen these days for instance, we have more material progress; more education; more humanity; more friendly and we are still progressing in the same direction.

The intellect of mankind is now as active as ever and is getting fresh knowledge as well as fresh experience every day to enable it to make still greater discoveries for instance in my point of view the discoveries of the future will far transcend the discoveries of the past.

I have discovered that the Geographical position; Climate; Food and Habits, all in time can change the character of human beings for instance, any white person emigrating into a low lying hot Tropical lands will become dark and his descendants in the course of ages will be Black because I believe the form and features are changed by the Geographical position.

In my research I also discovered that the missionaries turned the greatest savages into civilised man. The difference amongst mankind are more apparent than real for instance, when we see a person from another country with different features; different complexion; speaking different language; eating different food and believing in different religion. We are apt to think that he or she is quite different from ourselves, but it is only an ignorance.

CHAPTER 9

EVERY PERSON HAS THE RIGHT TO CULTIVATE LIFE

I discovered that, whenever a family or tribe divide and move far apart, different language dialects are formed and during ages it becomes a different language. For instance, when we watch the movie of Tarzan and how he was able to communicate with wild animals as he grew up amongst them and his language changed in the civilised society.

I think, one of the greatest requirements of mankind in the future will be a universal language so that any mankind on this earth will easily be able to converse with any other mankind as the world is getting more united as a result the want of a universal language is strongly felt hence I think there is sure to be one invented or adopted universal language and the question is: What language will that be?

In my point of view, I think English will be a suitable universal language because these days most people speak and understand in for instance in Europe, Africa, Asia, America and almost everywhere in the world. It is a composite and progressive language, and it is the language of a race that has intercourse with a far greater variety of nations than any other after Latin and Greek.

English is the language of the wealthiest, most powerful, most civilizing, most humanizing, most energetic, most progressive, and most cosmopolitan race the world ever saw. It has increased faster than French, Zulu, Sotho, Spanish, Xhosa, Chinese, Portuguese, and Italian all put together and is now beating them more than ever.

Throughout the vast Ebumnandini, English is being learnt through length and breadth of the country and is also being learnt to a great extent throughout the civilised world as a useful and necessary accomplishment. It is already pre - eminently the language of colonisation; commerce and literature thenceforth it has as much literature as all other languages put together.

Well! The language may be added to it or it may be improved or it may be enriched with the best and expressive words adopted from all other languages by learned men and women or by even International Congress of Experts which will be taught in every important or in all Government and Private Schools throughout the world as a useful accomplishment.

Bopa Lenna! Ke a kgumama ke bona e ka ha o nku tlwe ke a hweletsa ke bona e ka ha o mpone. Ke e ntseng se sebe pela mahlo a hao? Ke tswaletswe se beng e bile ke phela ha hara sona jwalo ka ha o itse sera sa hao phela le sona; eja le sona sebe se o bolaye. Mantswe a Hao ha motho ka a mamela ha ntle kappa a mamedisa ha ntle ha ho ya ka yang tse kong le Wena e bile re nere tla tlalwa ke tshabo le hlompho.

Morena ha o ntse o fa bana ba Hao bohobe sefete le lapa laka a ko bafe le bona hore ba tsebe hore o teng e bile o a phela ke mehla yohle. A ko ba rute botle le bobe; ba tsebe hore o ya phela ka hosa feleng. O bope le bona o ko o bafe toka le kgotso. Morena a ko nfe bo phelo nke ke hodise makgobunyane a o o nkadimeng ona; mohau Wa Hao ba holele ho Wena ba tsebe ho re o a phela.

Morena a ko qhalanye dira le meleko a tla nkgelosa ho o rapela. O tle o be le bona hara Meleko ya lefatshe lena. O ne wa re ke hodise bana empa bona ba I kgantshesa nna, A ko ke ne hara ho Motlotlwane o o onkileng wa kgethelo, wona ho re ke tla phela ka hare ho wona O tlise kgotso le mamello. Ke a tseba ke yona nako eo O ne wa e bo lela wa re Ke tla shapa Modisa dinku di tla qhalana di tlo hloka Modisana. Wa bua mantswe a thata Wa re Ke tla betsa lefatshe ka letjeketjane, Ke tla ba patisa ba ahi basa reng letho Ka Nna.

I made my resolution. Never again would I object to having a calf of mine taken away from me in the name of humanity. Death for me is clean and kind as well as merciful. For the first time in my life I realised that the great wisdom behind it all is the fact that I can see that life is hard and cruel but if we stay together, there is no strength in the world that could defeat us because when we are not afraid then we will be brave.

The whole world is outside, and may God love us and watch over us because the visitor which is death has crept in before me. It is not that I am well informed or smart but it is simply from study I have evolved and almost fool proof system for instance one that is simplicity itself and accepted generally any statement that seems reasonable and sensible, I simply say: "False or Incorrect."

I never bother to study the question on its merits because as for me that is waste of time because it may prompt me to go wrong. I realised that these fellows who make up the questions seem to have a knack of picking holes in all the established beliefs of humanity. The statement, "Cats can see in the dark "is obviously wrong to me because in my understanding women are worse drivers than men as most accidents are caused by them as a result of fear.

I have discovered that the only truly healthy person is a dead one because in my understanding "Healthy" means without ailments whatsoever and it also means devoid of such common Physiological symptoms as Ageing throng; the process of time and running low on energy due to exercise and suffering brain fatigue or sleepless from being awake hence I believe that, no living being or mechanism can exist without suffering ailments of one sort or another.

I have learnt that the present Law, both moral and legal in regard to suicide or euthanasia is obsolete and needs revision because an individual should be free to die and may even be taught that because sometimes it is his or her duty to die. Ultimately death will be restored to its long divinity.

I think if a man feels that life is becoming intolerable and desires to bring it to an end then the question for the Community to decide is whether his or her death would cause more suffering to relatives and friends than him or herself would suffer by living. If so, then suicide would not be allowed considering the fact that the individual has as much Right to die, provided it harms no other individual as to be born because any person has the right to cultivate life and strive for health and happiness.

It is the social and not the personal problem in which I am mainly interested because in my point of view, death is a social as it is really less problem concerned with self - destruction than with bringing the lives of others to an end . How many murders are committed in and around our country Ebumnandini per day? It is not one in which the medical profession can play a pioneering part since it is the business of medicine to prolong life and not to end it hence it has been discovered that Hypokalaemia is a condition that occurs when the body's potassium levels are low. One of the causes could be the long-term use of insulin to treat diabetes.

I believe in individualism that everyone has the Right to the Sacraments of such as air; the waters of love and of beauty; the right for life and the right of death. The time may come when it may be the Law that an individual may be sent to a merciful death which is not the Law at the present moment as neither the Magistrate nor Judge or Juror nor I have the Right to make Law. At the present time, those who commit "Merciful" killings are still charged for "Guilty Merciful or Guilty Insane. "

I did a little field - work on my own and I believe that, it is high time we have to take what we can get in such radical cases like mine hence I am the man who is willing to give my life for the struggling citizens of our country - Ebumnandini namely unemployed ; inmates with the so-called criminal records ; patients ; beggars to mention but few that they might be free . To accomplish my goal, I need to have one of the best defences any defendant could ever had because I cannot fight such a battle without money.

I fully disagree with the statement which says : "Dogs cannot climb trees" because in my research I discovered it has been disclosed that all dogs are capable of climbing trees like cats and that the reason they do not is because of an element in the bark of trees which is the Scenic Acid (fluid like acid found on the trunk and branches of trees) which is injurious to their feet and that if removed , dogs will climb like cats do for instance when we watch dogs participating in circuses or funny animals programmes on our televisions do.

I also discovered that it is not true that, Ducks like water because in my research I discovered that the Laboratory experiments conducted by Researchers; Scientists and other Experts have revealed the fact that, Ducks do not like anything and that they go in water purely to get away from Land which they dislike even more intensely than water.

Well! I carried my Cross and made the best of everything. It was hard but I did it because most of us today call a spade a spade. Even though we do not refer to a girl or woman's legs as limbs but a man gets thoughts off his chest and is done with them but a woman is not equally permitted to get thoughts off her mind and these that remain to crawl about with their increasing slimy warmness. Men usually outgrows their taste for pornography after they have completed at an early age whereas women's taste for pornography seems seldom to abate.

It came to my realisation that fear is a mental hazard of crossing our bridges before we come to them hence fear or panic caused by fear is responsible for at least ninety percent of all accidents. It is a mistake to believe that men are always hunters and women always be prey because the love instinct in women is not a simple thing but a complex structure composed of many elements rooted deep in a woman's unconscious, hence every men must symbolically play the four roles of being a Father; Brother; Lover and Child to every woman.

It is false to say: "It is lighter in the daytime than at night because all the light we get on this planet - Earth comes from the Sun. The Sun gives just as much light all the time even at night just as much as in the daytime. It is just as light at night, but we just do not see it hence women think of sex in the daytime as well as at night.

According to sales statistics based on my research, it has been disclosed women of all ages are chief consumers of cheap sex novels and the Magazines and these led me to ask myself the following question:" Does cold air look any different than any other kind of air?" Sex for me must be articulated like hatred as it can produce a disturbing internal malaise. With what I experienced in my life especially when the light of respect for me had begun to fade, I was pretty near my boiling point but later I realised that the score is one to nothing in favour of me.

I sometimes wonder whether these learner - girls with their instigator who orchestrated them are really big enough for the role they played for putting me and my family in this evil and dangerous situation or whether they actually are worthy of their good fortune because time to me is of essence . How can we be sure that, when we close the door of the refrigerator, the light it, turns off?

According to Psych gynaecology which is the Science of understanding women, there is a distance between men and women which is Biological and Psychological. Women for instance try to pretend they have not done it or thought it and they cannot bear to admit it even to themselves. Let alone to me but it is coming nearer and nearer to the surface. Things are not always good or bad and for that, people cannot just label things Black or White because there are Greys and lots of colours.

CHAPTER 10

WHO AM I TO COMPLAIN WHEN THE GOOD CHRIST WAS CRUCIFIED?

The nearer they came to a solution of their problem, the harder they fought against the cure. It must have slipped my mind that women are always turning instinctively to men like their fathers. If they do not like it here in Umhlola Townships due to various jobs I adorned at one time or another, why do not they go back where they came from instead of corrupting our Area. Well! If they do not move, the bees will sting them.

A strange mysterious feeling had shivered in me on the day of the incident which nearly forces me on all fours because there is little use in the male trying to fight the seductive, she-devil with a firehose. Well!

Seeing is believing hence I realised that males grow to adulthood in the bashful blind belief that the females from Divine (females are from Divine meaning they are spiritually blessed). To my surprise, it was I who was doing the complaining and they were trying to cheer up but shuddered as if they had been caught in a lie.

I was wracking my brains to find some means of helping them because I know when women together, they talk and breed trouble hence I was a soft prey of such frauds because the subject has the alluring danger of a "Wet Paint" sign but it was difficult to keep my hands off from doing what is right despite all warnings. These has taught me that, costumes for the female figure (their natural physical bodies) are doing more than any other factors in civilisation to destroy man's faith in the finer things of life.

My experience has taught me to realise that, when a girl is first turned loose in the world of men , the game of seduction is win or lose or draw which is pretty exciting but she does not yet know the pain of living and I can assure you that she will soon learn although she is very pretty. Seduction for me should be above all things, glamorous and exciting because sex to me is something which Nature has implanted in all of us and in its proper relation to life is a very beautiful thing.

It was brought to my attention that she had been advised by someone who knew to come to me because she seemed to fear and respect me. She was under some sort of surveillance which means she was exposed only occasionally and for a brief periods of time and not the extensive and intensive campaigns she'll have to face when she becomes what is so quaintly known as bachelor girl.

I have been able to order my own meals and I think I will continue to do so. When I am hungry, I will eat but if the proper food is available and no one is going to force improperly prepared food on me when I am not hungry. I am not those men who sit with their backs to the streets because they will eye every women who passes and spend too much time on the subject of sex as they devote their lives to it by talking it; reading it; singing it and does everything but do it.

As a teacher I taught well because I love it. I know how to listen as well as to talk because I believe in quantity and not quality hence to see my learners and students is to love them. I have fought winds and cold and the devil himself could not break his tail any harder than I and my family here in our so-called democratic country – Ebumnandini.

Who am I to complain when the good Christ Himself was crucified? I am not afraid or have any fear of them whether they send the evil eye to my home before I put my foot. Is it not possible to breathe God's air without fear of dominating the pall of unemployment? My training thought quickly took in my family; home and hopes but with hope came fear. Dear Lord, guide my path to be in the home and not of the home.

O tla dumellana le nna ha kere ha le fete kgomo le je Motho. Batho be so mamelang ha ke le jwetsa ke le supisa tsela hobane re ba eti mona le fatsheng lena. Lefatshe lena ke le mpetje e bile ke le tshwantsha le lebidi la koloi kappa koloi hobane ha o tsebe mohlang e tla o diha. Lefatshe lena ke le tshwantsha le moruwi ho dima le fatshe hoba ha hona seo a se hlokang. Ha ntse a phela ha are letho ka Modimo, seo a se hopolang ke maruo a hae a lefatshe. Mohlang Monga bophelo a mohopolang o a tseba hore Modimo o teng.

Bana baka hlompho ke ntho ya pele ho mang kapa mang a e kokobetsang ka mehla hobane le ya bona hore dintho di fetohile ha di sa tshwana le dinako tseo re neng re hola ka tsona. Batho ba tsohelana matla; Ban aba tla fetohela batswadi ba bona empa ke re ho lona holang le sena ditokelo tsa le fatshe lena hobane ha dina thuso.

Fadimehang ke hona le be bohlale ho bona tse mpeho na le ho kena ho tsona. Lefatshe le ha hlamisitse molomo wa lona ho kwenya ba le kgahlisang ka mesebetsi ya satane. Mamelang kgalemo honale menate ya le fatshe e senang meputso ho lona. Bana baka ha ke rialo ha ke bui le ho lona fela, empa ke bau le ba i kobetsang melao ya Batswadi ba bona, ba dumelang hore kgalemo ke ntho eteng. Tshabang kgalemo!

I give you this advice “Free of Charge “You are not a failure until you start blaming others for your mistakes. When one door closes another door opens but we often look so long and so regretfully upon the closed door that we do not see the ones which open for us, hence, in my study I learnt that the home is a woman’s most challenging and fertile field.

I discovered that all men are essentially diggers that is grave diggers; sewerage diggers; farmers digging potatoes ; Doctors digging into people's bellies and so on and when as a man, you dig down at the certain level, you suddenly evolve from a common digger to a miner hence I believe in no one but myself because I realised that most people spend far more time in words than in action.

I still saw my world darkening when the ever last lifted and the stars were there as before but I wasn't trapped; I wasn't helpless and I was free and I didn't have to shout or commit suicide to show them. All these experiences have led me to freedom from anger and fear which resulted for me to freedom to know happiness and love hence the scales had dropped from my eyes and I could see life in its proper perspective. It seems nothing had changed and yet everything had changed.

Before I had any real opportunity to give, I had to learn the equally important lesson of receiving graciously as I was accepting help with one hand and pushing it away with the other hence I was always at odds with the entire Education and Justice Departments , not to say the country as a whole. I was out of step with life; with my family and with people in general because I made everybody near and dear to me because everybody seemed to be picking on me but I could not be suicidal at my age hence I was thrown in jail being innocent as I am.

OH! Our Father who art in Heaven, grant me the serenity to accept the things I cannot change and courage to change the things I can as well as the wisdom to know the difference because I believe, no individual can carry all the burdens of this world.

Nothing has happened to me do I deserve. I am talking about the good things that have happened. Society can do anything it chooses to do with me but there go my good intentions; fear of consequences; will care and the responsibility for my behaviour.

I learnt that, the only real freedom a human being can ever know is doing what he or she ought to do because you want to do it because God works through people maybe for me to be locked behind bars for so long wasn't God's time yet and to be released as I expected but I believed that the time will come at His time and will.

It is stated that two - thirds of the men who are in Prisons were under the influence of alcohol or drugs when they committed their offences and they reverted to the old ways of life we know, which is the life full of anger; resentment; fear; dependence; denial and so on hence they find themselves back in Prisons where their personalities become even more waved. I would not only find a way to live without having a drink, but I would find a way to live without wanting to drink if I were them.

In my study I learned that, if we have resentment, we want to be free of and that if we pray for the person or a thing that we resent then we will be free. If we will ask in prayer for everything, we want ourselves to be given us or them, we will be free. Ask for their health; their prosperity; their happiness and we will be free. Even when we do not really want it for them and our prayers are only words and we do not mean it, let us go ahead and do it anyway.

When we do it every day, we will find that we have come to mean it and to want it for them. We will then realise that, where we used to feel bitterness, resentment, and hatred, we now feel compassionate understanding and love because we cannot live with anger.

I did the right things in the wrong way and I am willing to right all the wrongs I have ever done to anyone, no matter how wrong I thought the others were. OH

LORD! Let your light shine so before us, that we may see your good works. I am willing to be honest with myself about myself and I am willing to think of other people; of their needs instead of myself in order to get rid of my problems , and when I do then all my troubles will be over .

Cold chills started chasing up and down my spine; my teeth were chattering and my hands were shaking, so I tucked them under me to keep them from flying away because no one likes to look at a pretty woman better than like I do and my mouth waters like a pump when I see them hence together we get along like a couple of old side - kicks. I know that sounds conceited as the devil darn it, but it is true.

On the other hand, it makes my heart bleed to think of some men enslaved by the woman's eyes, that they are blinded by the golden sunshine of their hair in such a way that they would cut off their right arms for them because when these women are good, they are superlatively so. Their motto is always “Fool them and forget them.”

I suppose no one ever has the heart to tell all men in our country - Ebumnandini that we should have our cakes and eat them too. In my research I discovered that to some women these days, love is a game of chess because now it is your move and now again is mine. If you do this, I’ll do that and if she says that, it means I should do this hence I refer to them as Talkers and not Doers.

I have also discovered that some of the crudest men ply women with alcohol until they lose control. In my point of view, this technique is so bad as it does not merit serious discussion and the woman who succumbs to this attack is completely foolish especially those who are particularly light-headed drinkers and potential nymphomaniacs.

Such people tend to forget that there are many things worse than dying. Is there any death worse than the progressive, self-induced, and slow suicide of practicing alcoholic? In my understanding, Alcohol wrings the guts out of life; eats the brain in such a way as to make an Alcoholic blind to the truth. Some of them hear voices when none is around and see things which are not there.

Whilst behind bars I got off the hook and my mind began to clear off the fog that covered it and I realised that alcohol is no respecter of Economic status; social and business standing or intelligence hence it had become a crutch and a means of retreat from life. Despite great opportunities, alcohol nearly ended most people's lives.

Today alcohol only reaches men's stomachs and their subconscious minds, getting very chatting and open – mouthed as well as to perspire about their foreheads and women pleases them with no cold and static beauty. I discovered that women who laugh easily are easy to love even if they are not exciting, meaning physically disturbing. It came to my realisation that the day house or brothel has many entrances but just one exists. It is easy to get in but so hard to get out hence I resorted to watch and wait for an opportunity to get out and this requires diplomacy and tact.

Chapter 11

LIFE IS REAL AND EARNEST

I learnt that the education and justice departments in our country as well as some community members who were and still are against me were happy about the outcomes of my labour and court hearings and were voicing my growing pains but the hands that create are attached to warm hearts and not to calculating minds.

What I experienced has taught me about acceptance. That acceptance is the key to my relationship with God. I never just sit and do nothing while waiting for Him to tell me what to do. Rather I do whatever is in front of me to be done and I will leave the results up to Him, hopefully that is God's will for me.

Acceptance of things as they are having replaced the old impatient champing at the bit to conquer the world and courage to face each day has replaced the fears and uncertainties of earlier years.

Living just for today is a pleasant adventure but there comes a time when a person does not want to live and is afraid to die hence, I kept myself busy, always have something constructive to do. Who am I to say there is no God?

God! Here I am and here are all my troubles. I have made a mess of things and can't do anything about it. You take me and all my troubles and do anything you want with me!

Do you know what happens when you feed charcoal to a fire and fan the flame? For things we never mention; for art misunderstood and for excellent intention that did not turn good hence most men talk of crime and thieving; wrote of fraud and lies to save our injured feelings. It was on me like a thunderclap which racked me through and through.

Speaking in general, I have tried them all and found them good for such as one cannot use one bed too long due to the happy roads that take us men over the world. I discovered that, sleeping with a woman is one of the arts which is the art of self-defence; sometimes totally unprepared for what happens to us because we are plunged by tradition into the unaided battle of the bedroom, armed only with the most meagre previous experience.

We men may fight valiantly at the routine beginning but eventually one and all find ourselves weakened refugees from the coveted regions of the rest. We are babies in a bedroom which leads to the sleeping killing tactics of women which has become purely force habit which has also become a constant routine.

I have discovered in my research that; no deep feelings would be aroused by this physiological need even though there is nothing like it under the sun. You hear an age - old cry of a man in the night: "My God, I've got to get some sleep." Thereafter the struggle for sleep is immediate and unending.

It all started after millions of words have been spoken and written on human love experiences but the wealth of information steps right there. Yes! It is reasonable to suppose that every organism requires certain juices to complete and maintain itself and such relationships are not based on sexual pleasure but on to exchange of perfectly assorted liquid.

I have discovered that in our so-called democratic country - Ebumnandini, beautiful women are able to eat men and spit their bones into the earth's hole by using their champagne movements which can be accomplished only by human female; for instance, a lovely girl makes pleasant and cheerful scene and she confers a favour upon each person who sees her.

People especially us men look at her because the sight of her pleases us. The faster she hurries; the faster she jiggles, meaning what happens with her body when she walks; turns; bends; reaches or stamp her foot. Everybody especially us men see and enjoy it but, in my understanding, only God approves it hence with advancing years the jiggle becomes a menace, and a woman is in grave danger of flying to pieces.

Seeing all these, I resorted to an old trick to make both men and women feel more at ease but I can't make them both stand trial if they want to plead guilty because I realised that a kiss or two permitted in a moment of weakness does not exactly establish the fact that they are willing to turn over their beautiful bodies for that, therefore a man or woman have to get him or herself a new approach and really his or her path will be paved with recumbent maidens or unmarried males , as repetition is so boring to himself or herself and a character of a wench he or she is lusting for. I refer to both men and women because of equal rights if they really exist in our so-called democracy as it always preached in our lives.

In my experience I have seen men who starts on a "Just friends" approach to women, worms their way into a woman's heart. Such men are referred to as big brother because they are very sweet; sympathetic and understanding. They play a waiting game but when they put pressure, the woman is defenceless.

In my study I learnt that, there are those women who are referred to as being psychologically mature who believe that, being a woman is neither a sign of inferiority nor of superiority but they want to be comrades complements and not ornaments. They want to share both the privilege and responsibilities of freedom. They neither want to cling to a man and play weak sisters. They do not want to parade masculinity by expressing their mannishness but demands that their own Spirits and Independence be acknowledged for their worth. I personally regard such women, women of the future because to me they are most satisfactory; the most thrilling; the most completely human women to have; the hardest to get and the most difficult to hold.

I am biding my time by doing more and more research concerning everything pertaining our lives. That is the kind of guy I am hence I have discovered that there are those women who are known as mattress fighters or 'can't get settled' types because they continually wrestle the mattresses, no matter in what position they try to find sleep, that position seems uncomfortable for instance when they get into bed , they'll stretch quietly at full length for a moment and suddenly they'll hurtle sideways; twisting themselves into an acute letter "S", and they can heave from flat back to stomach with agility or spread themselves over the bed . For all of that, they are the commonly recognised disturbers of masculine sleep.

Have you ever heard of a cat-and-mouse attack between men and women? You'll hear a man say to a woman: "I don't love you and I know, you don't love me, but I can't help wanting you. Why pretend?"
You will also hear him say: "If I continue to see you, I'll make love to you."
Such a guy will never use force; never put any obvious pressure to a woman before safety. That is his motto.

I also discovered when courting a Revolutionary Stream woman is to court eternal conflict unless as a man , you desire to spend the rest of your days in a dog - and - cat conflict for prestige because it is said these type of women need men to always help them with their coats ; give them flowers and perfumes as gifts . Their men should not fail to be nice to their Mothers; always take them to Church and imitate their Fathers.

The life is real, and life is earnest. Opportunity knocks but once, so grab each fleeing moment while you may school as one Philosopher once said: "Men should have an art of understanding women or else ..."hence there are those men who are physical and goes to the root of the matter; attacks women with body blows and they explain at great length that, sex is an appetite which must be satisfied if a man isn't to become a victim of all sorts of fetishes and suppressed desires.

God gave all men all earth to love but since our hearts are small and ordained for each one spot then it should prove beloved over all hence there are those women who are said to be old - fashioned because they still believe in their inferiority as women and the superiority of men over them. They want to learn on a strong man, and they demand that they be treated chivalrously and protected as if they are a delicate and frail flower incapable of existence in a hard and matter of fact world.

The Revolutionary Stream women on the other hand rejects this old theory because they themselves are aggressive; independence; mannish and go - getting. They often insist that they are far better than men because they want to pay as they go and be treated like men.

Have you ever heard of the women who are known as the Pillar lookers? There is nothing disturbing for a man than realise that the woman lying beside him in the darkness is fully awake and looking in his direction. They are almost the same as the women whom I regard as the Inching rollers who can be elbowed; shouted at and kicked but they keep on inching with unabated vigour and remarkable placidity and a man must choose between yelling like a lumber jack or walking stealthily around to the lately departed other side.

All that our forefathers taught us of old, pleases us now no more hence women are now more powerful than men in almost all spheres of life especially in the bedroom where the brides of Frankenstein yell at their men for instance by saying: "When in hell are you going to get in bed?" Their annoying prelude to sleep involves long intervals in front of the bathroom mirror and the dressing table. Face creams are rubbed on, then rubbed off before approaching the bed at her own time.

Have you ever heard of the Twitchers who are also known as Jerky One? Such women maybe the picture of physical health and mental serenity, yet at the slightest touch or noise, they'll twitch in their sleep and they'll sit suddenly straight up in bed, taking the covers with them and they are addicted to dealing out short rabbit kicks in conjunction with their jerking.

If a man can wait and not tired by waiting or being lied about. I suggest that he must not deal with lies or being hated and he must not give way to hating and yet he must not look too good nor talk too wise. As a man, don't think highly of individualism when courting women as the pagan men do by insisting that today we see sexual relationship with a new vision; a proper perspective as they say to women: "After all we want each other, what is there to stop us?" "Aren't we free people; free to live our own lives?"

I realised that, some men come to a woman bearing gifts which are generally expensive and tendered of which is possible for the semi - prostitute to accept the wages without feeling too professional because those gifts have sound economic and not emotional basis. For that reason, it is liable to work with any of the women who have not been born heiresses.

The law by which we live is that we are not built to comprehend a lie; we can neither love nor pity nor forgive hence we have men who try to get the women through passionate declarations of love and they may even plead to marry a woman even it is too soon but the women who have been around will merely enjoy their laugh when approached and promptly send them back to the minor leagues where they belong and to them such men are called the cheapest.

The longest arm, the sharpest tooth gave man control of man; gave woman control of woman and woman of man and vice versa hence we have women who vacillate , who want privileges of emancipation without its responsibilities and they are hopelessly involved in the age - old problem of having their cake and eating it too which has resulted to Ham-eist, who are misunderstood husbands, as married men are seldom worth the trouble. Advice freely given is that women should send such men home to their wives in short order as there is no elucidation needed. Boys will be boys and men will be men.

All that our hearts bid us to believe, we doubt where we do not deny. On that note I have discovered other women who are grouped as Eternal Glamorists because going to bed is to them a ceremony because they have a flair for good - looking night - gowns; lounging robes and there are no oily creams or head gears for them. They always look their best and they like to sit on the edge of the bed for a last cigarette. They trail around the room talking brightly about very and they will not relax even in bed. They go right on posturing, talking and being glamorous with fatiguing intensity.

CHAPTER 12

THOUGHT IS MARRIED TO THOUGHT AND PRODUCES OTHER THOUGHTS

Have you ever heard of the neck nosers who are most irritating and hardest to curb? These women cleave to conquer. Their devilish art of sleeping begins with the slipping of a casual arm over the chest of the unfortunate guy who happens to be at their side. Next few moments, she settles a soft chin quite definitely upon the man's weary shoulder. Her final gesture is a short upward tug accompanied by a slight inward heave. Her face rests in the hollow of his unwilling neck and the wisps of stray hair begin to tickle his nostrils with deadly insistence.

When sleeping next to the women who are bed readers, the sharp thudding of a book to the floor at any time in the night, the rustle of a sheaf of magazine. Wo He! If the man moves any part of his tired anatomy, the ready for debate attitude which is an unfairly signal verbal combat. May our love create our earth and see that it is good. Each to her choice and I rejoice because I realised that the women who are Mush boilers when asleep, their breath is inhaled through the nose , then exhaled into the mouth with a slight puffing of the cheeks and sometimes the exhalation is accompanied by a faint whistling sound.

When nature in her nakedness defeats us every time, it is not learning or grace nor gear and it is not easy meat nor drink but bitter pinch of pain and fear that makes creation think the race is run by one and one and never by two and two . I can dream and not make dreams my master. I can think and not make thoughts my aim hence I had a love on earth that kissed me to my fall because I have taken my fun where I have found it, and now I must pay for it.

The earth is full of anger; the Seas are dark with wrath. The Nations are in their harness; proud hearts; rebellious brows; deaf ears and soul uncaring as a result to the safety for the rich and danger for the poor.

Train up a child! Perhaps it means to train only the little girls and let the boys run wild. Well! Be patient boys, the time will come when we shall be all men. And when it does, I think wrongs will be righted then, for instance Girl Graduates wear gowns precisely like those worn by University men and made by the same Tailor. The only way to tell which from the other, is to wait for a mouse.

I learnt that if you talk to a woman about religion and she sighs. When talking to her of love, she simpers. Talk to her of Art and she yawns; talk to her of Science and she goes to sleep but talk to her of dress, she will open her eyes and give you the entire attention of her ears.

Courting on the other hand is a luxury. The man who has never courted has lived in vain. Men fall ill of love or fail in love at the young age. The signs of sickness are quite plain. The unfortunate men usually lose their appetite; they wear their Sunday clothes all the year round; they usually become moody; they give short answers to their elders and they also regard their friends as Brutes.

When in love I discovered also in my research that such men cannot endure to eat delicious food. Their chief diet is the nectar of the woman's lips and the music of her voice. When such man is away from her, they appear unhappy but when he is in the same room with her, he hangs his head on one side and drawls when he speaks and sits on the edge of a chair. It is also said such men continually talk about their misery.

Kiss can only be described by taking one, then set down all alone out of the draft and smack your lips. Kissing is one of those few things that is easier done than described.

Education in my understanding means instruction in everything which human beings have done, thought, or discovered, for instance all languages, History and Sciences. When comparing two systems of education from each, the expected results may be equally extravagant. The way of it lies through Industrial teaching where the practical underlies the intellectual hence the millions must never be condemned to toil their hands, or the race will cease to exist. In my understanding as an Educator, to educate successfully, one should first ascertain clearly with sharp and distinct outline what one means by an educated human being.

Education is for making educated human beings. An educated human being in my point of view, is human being whose intelligence has been cultivated and who knows something of the world he or she lives in. Maybe during my schooling days, they have been feeding me with chips of granite and these may have led me to arrange my letters into words and each became a thought. A symbol waking in my mind an image of a real thing by grouping my words into sentences hence thought is married to thought and produces other thoughts therefore the chips of granite becomes soft bread which is wholesome; nutritious and invigorating.

Education these days is in every body's lips but for me an Action is a real Teacher because if you require much, you must produce much and if you produce little, you must require little. If you are rich in mind, you are expected to be poor in body hence our learners and students had to carry their wardrobes on their backs to seek or pursue knowledge even though the tuition fees are hardest and the boarding or lodging is the barest.

It came to my realisation that being able to do something and not merely to answer questions must still be a backbone of education of everybody who has to earn his or her bread by manual labour hence no education which does not make its first aim , is worth anything at all . Our great Schools: Colleges and Universities are currently in the middle of a revolution. Most revolutions are indicating and revealing discontent with what we have with no clear idea of what we would have. Even ourselves cannot have wholly escaped the infection, if we have then we will not escape it long.

I suggest that the Universities and Colleges in Mzansi – South Africa should be devoted to spiritual cultures and assume its present character in consequence. They should teach the accompanying necessary lesson of poverty. Students must be taught to endure hardship because every human being, no matter of what grade or calling should learn handicraft than the human of intellect because in my opinion, it hurts no intellect to be able to make a house or a pair of shoes. If you can do either of those, you have nothing to fear from fortune. I will rather work with my hands and keep my brain for myself because to do what I do well, should be the first thing; the salaries or wages should be the second and the rewards are in proportion to his or her skill as well as Industry hence the best Carpenter has to receive the highest pay.

The Students should learn at the Tertiary Institutions like Universities what will enable them to earn their living as soon after they leave it as possible because if all those precious years are wasted on what is useless will never be learnt properly at all. History; Poetry; Philosophy and other Courses are excellent as Ornaments and if we care for such things, they may be the amusement of our leisure hereafter but they will not help us to stand on our feet and walk on our own. For this reason, no one shall properly be a man until we can do that.

There is no direction in which our own Subjects or Learning Areas or Courses will not lead us if we care to follow them to the furthest boundary of thought. If we should teach our Learners or Students Subjects or Learning Areas or Courses which they can only remember mechanically then we teach them nothing which is worth their while to know.

We should teach them Facts and Principles which they can apply and use in the work of their lives, for instance, the best Lawyer and the best Doctors command most practice and make the largest fortunes.

A person cannot learn everything because the Objects of Knowledge have multiplied beyond the powers of the strongest mind to keep pace with them all. You must choose among them and the only reasonable guide to choose in such matters is Utility. If for example a Doctor; a Lawyer; a Handicraft man and others has it in him or her to become a great person, he or she can ascend through his or her profession to any height to which his or her talents are equal. The challenge is only that, he or she starts a great many rounds higher up the ladder. What I deplore in our higher education is the devotion of so much effort and so many precious years to subjects or Learning Areas or Courses which have no practical bearing upon life.

The present rule on which Authors are paid is by the page and the sheet. The more words the more pay. Great Scientific discovery; Great Poetry; Every Intellectual production which has genius work and performance in it, is the fruit of long thought and patient as well as painful collaboration hence the work of this kind done hastily would be better not be done at all.

Before we begin to build, let us have a plan of a house that we would construct because in our civilised and artificial Communities, there are many ways where Fools have money and Rogues want it by effecting a change of possession. Experience is no more transferable in morals than in art because the drawing Master can direct his or her pupil generally in the principle of Art and he or she can teach him or her here and there, to avoid familiar stumbling blocks but the pupil must realise every rule which the Master gives him or her.

In my research, I have learnt about the primeval chaos saying: "Let there be light!" Light! Yes, because according to my understanding we want light, but it must be the Light which will help us to work and find Food and Clothes and a Place for ourselves. First and foremost, we have to earn our living and all the "'ologies" will not by themselves enable us to earn it.

Instruction does not prevent waste of time or mistakes. Mistakes themselves are often the best

Teachers of all. Action on the other hand is a real Teacher. We know what was good but would not do it. My misfortune was that I was not looking beyond the point of my Shoes because I cared nothing for the future and less for the past.
The truth is plain as the Sun because I had to bid the dead virtues live again and plant the eternal rules in the consciences of the people. I think, it is simple because the difficulty was not to know what to do but how to do it.

I therefore pass this message to our so-called "Democratic Government of Mzansi" to inform all our neighbouring Countries as well as those abroad to send us no more of what we regard as "Educated people" but to send us Smiths; Carpenters; Masons; Mechanics; Plumbers ...and all these will thrive because for me Educated people are a log in our hands as they loaf in uselessness till their means are spent.

My rhetoric Question to you as a Reader is: “What will you choose between a Ball point and Pencil when writing a letter to the people you love most or when you apply for a job?” I believe that Readers are Leaders. Truly old people hit the target by saying we should not cut down trees which offer us shade or pollute water which we will need for drinking.

It is said:” Failure plus Persistence equals Success hence I am not judged by the number of times I fail but by the number of times I succeed and the number of times I succeed is in direct proportion to the number of times I fail and keep trying. If things start going wrong, having a consistent approach prevents panic. Do not change the way you do things because of pressure. The things you choose to do, tell a lot about you as a person and the way to be nothing is to do nothing.

The only place where success comes before work is in the Dictionary. Work is the cause and success are the effect. Do not avoid difficult things just because you are afraid to make mistakes. Every obstacle is simply a course to develop your achievement muscle and for that reason, one should look at obstacles or problems as challenges that make one stronger by not letting them to stop you. Problems that get in the way, only test your willingness in all your efforts which simply means, being on the tight rope is living and everything else is waiting.

The only time a person does not fail is the last he or she tries anything. It works by showing others what you think is important through your actions, because through positive actions, you can make the world a better place. Positive words encourage positive actions and for that reason, you must never discourage anyone who continually makes progress, no matter how slow because it is said due to union, the smallest parties thrives but as a result of discord the greatest are destroyed.

CHAPTER 13

WHAT DO WE LOSE IF WE TRY THE HARDEST?

Failure is part of learning just like making mistakes lead us to understand how to do things better and take on larger and more complex challenges. Mistakes are opportunities to learn and improve. Success on the other hand is the ability to go from one failure to another with no loss of enthusiasm. Never let the fear of striking out get in your way because risks exit in everything, we try. I discovered that, every event has a cause, and that one event stimulates a result that would not have occurred without the initial cause hence the way to becoming great is to do great. Do not be afraid of trying new things because doing new things stretches our minds to be able to take on new challenges.

It is better to be prepared for an opportunity and not have one than to have an opportunity and not be prepared because what lies behind us and what lies before us are tiny matters compared to what lies within us.

Patience serve as a protection against wrongs as clothes do against cold thus a problem on the other side is a chance for us to do our best. I discovered in my research that a person who does not try is worse off than the person who fails hence inspiration exists, but it must find us working. It is by acts and not by ideas that we live. My questions is:" What do we lose if we try the hardest?" Most of the time, we lose nothing, but we gain everything. In my understanding it is easier to keep going than it is to get started hence I stopped thinking and started writing.

I discovered that those who do not tell the truth may think they have an advantage for a moment but in the end, most lies are discovered and people would hesitate to trust someone who had lied in the past. Lying can never save us from another lie because once a person lies, there will ultimately be other lies to assist the first lie. Lying may seem easier than facing the truth but one lie often leads to more trouble in the future because lies hurt others and lead to more lies.

Have you ever been tempted to lie about something that happened to avoid getting into trouble? Mahatma Gandhi once said: “Truth never damages a cause that is just.” In my understanding he meant that, if a person gets in trouble, the best thing a person can do is to tell the truth about what happened.

If others lie, they will only have more problems and continue to get in trouble. Do not worry about anyone else getting in trouble because we are what we repeatedly do. Excellence then is said to be not an act but a habit.

Have you ever noticed how both good and bad things happen on the same day? Let us take a lesson from the trees and watch the way they learn to bend with each breeze. Breeze may come from one side and then another, like problems that can come up out of nowhere. The secret is to always do our best regardless of which direction the breeze is blowing because the situation can change in an instant, just as the tree learns to bend with each breeze. By so doing we can be ready for something good to happen after something bad has happened. To achieve that we should have positive attitude which helps good things happen to us hence a person is responsible for his or her choice and must accept consequences whatever they may be.

In my studies I learnt that "Respect" has to do with how we look at things. "Re" means "Again" and "Spect" has to do with how we look at things hence "glasses" are referred to as "Spectacles." Spectacular on the other hand means something amazing to look at. In my understanding, to respect means to look at something again in a special way. If we respect others, then other people will look at us as special people. I discovered that, by doing good things for others then we are like the honeybee that makes the world beautiful. I believe that the Time is always right to do what is right and when others notice the good things, we do, they are inspired to follow our good example.

It has been discovered that, to take the first step for most of us is a frightening thing and to face the unknown brings uncertainty. It is like the child who is tired to crawl, the first step is the most important of all because it expands his or her horizons thereafter a child or we can see a new light and the joy of discovery is like taking a flight. I learnt also that, the first step we take will open all doors and to see ourselves as we have seen ourselves before, but we only just need to be brave enough to take the first step.

I therefore suggest that we as fellow citizens of Mzansi should keep away from people who try to belittle our ambitions. For instance, small people always do that, but the great people make us feel that we too can be great.

I discovered that, people who make fun of other people's goals don't do great things themselves and those who tease are jealous of the amazing things that other people accomplish hence they are afraid of those who make great attempts because they are reminded that they lack ambition themselves and for that, let us show them that, we want to develop the habit of excellence by listening and doing all our work every day.

The temptation to slack off starts when we are feeling good about who we are and what we have achieved. After we have spent ourselves emotionally and physically to achieve the great dream, it is easy to accept the illusion that the struggle has ended. Let us not allow anything to distract us because if we stop, the results will be less than spectacular or there may be no results at all. Whenever something stands in our way and makes our lives difficult , we must realise that , the harder we work to overcome it , the greater our success will we feel hence it is said :"The greater the obstacle , the greater the glory in overcoming it."

Dreams; Ideas and Possibilities exist inside everyone and are just waiting to emerge hence Courage is required to do things others don't think we can do hence it is clearly stated that:" Courage is resistance to fear; Master of fear and not the absence of fear. It has also been discovered that, Success is said to be ninety nine percent failure thus trying new things means you will probably make mistakes but the essential thing is not to have conquered but to have fought well and that you just reach a point where if you don't do it , you'll regret it.

It was brought to my attention that, the most important thing in Olympic Games is not to win but to take part therefore the most important thing in life is not the triumph but the struggle. Everything we see today was made by past Generation and before its appearance, it was a Thought in the mind of a person or an impulse in the heart of a human being.

Even after a bad harvest, there must be sowing hence it is a rough road that leads to the heights of greatness. A person must find the desire to succeed within him or herself. Even if you have achieved great success, look for new challenges that will keep you motivated to achieve greater and greater heights but you must be bold enough to revise and re-try your projects because to be prepared is half the victory. Remember! Effort is the key to getting the great results you want hence it is said: "The greater the effort, the greater the success " and at the end, you will be happy when you are enjoying what you are doing.

If everyone uses his or her talents to help others on daily basis, the world would be a better place. Remember! No one can do the work for you and No one can make you want to give your best because an example is not the main thing in influencing others, but it is the only thing. I am a great believer in "Luck", and I find out that the harder you work, the more you have of it because Luck comes regularly to those who work hard. All these made me realise that people who do not give up become more successful.

If we are not learning and growing, boredom sets in but by working hard and not giving up, will make us continually Lucky and successful as we face new challenges. Even if we are good on something, we must continue to improve and expand ourselves. If a person thinks he or she is going to succeed, he or she will because success seems to be largely a matter of hanging on, after others have let go. I realised that, if a problem is very difficult, most people tend to give up but only the person who is most persistent will be successful one to discover the solution.

We are not put on this Earth for ourselves but are placed here for each other. If you are always there for others, then in time of need, someone will be there for you like a tree you have planted and watered, the tree will grow. My free advice to my fellow countrymen is that, we should never do something good with the expectation of receiving some payment or benefit from our efforts because people naturally want to respond to good deeds by doing good deed in return.

Never look where you are going, always look where you want to go because in the middle of difficulty lies an opportunity. When you decide to do something, perform one small action and suddenly it is a tide then the momentum is going and there is no possibility of turning back hence you should start by doing what is necessary then what is possibly and suddenly you will be doing the impossible because we learn the most from the challenges we are facing.

As each year passes in Schools; Colleges; Universities or Work, we, and our fellow learners; students or colleagues are expected to master a year's worth of lesson or work. The challenges naturally become greater as we continue to the following year by moving from elementary levels to secondary levels. We cannot expect our work to be easier because if it did, we would not be challenged at an increasing higher level.

Our progress can be measured through our ability to handle more and more difficult problems hence Henry Kissinger stated: "Each success only buys an admission ticket to a more difficult problem." In my understanding, each success enhances our skills and puts us in a position to take on more complex problems.

I discovered that our brains are like the muscles in our bodies because they get stronger and stronger with use and that a mind stretched by a new idea never returns to its original dimension. It clearly stated that , first comes the idea and then come the actions that bring ideas into reality as a result we 'll get what we expect and should expect success because the human spirit needs to accomplish to achieve; to triumph and to be happy.

A good name is better than riches because having a good name means that people can respect and trust you. Everything we do contributes to what others think of us because our actions help people decide what they think of us. We are therefore obliged to show that we have good qualities which will make us to have a good name, among others.

I realised that, building a good reputation is very difficult when doing things that harm others but doing things one knows are wrong, will not make one feel good about oneself and that will let one down. When a person gives in to pressure from others, he or she will only feel good when he or she do what is right.

Though no one can go back and make a brand new start but anyone can start from now and make a brand new ending by getting around the right people ; associate with positive and goal - oriented people who encourage and inspire you that , by helping others makes you happier and healthier . Whatever you do, do it with all you might because creativity is so delicate a flower that praise tends to make a bloom but Discouragement on the other hand often nips it in the bud. Furthermore, it is said, Incredible dreams help people see that the impossible can sometimes be achieved by merely conquering your own thoughts and doubts by keeping working towards a goal no one had yet achieved.

In my research I also discovered that, Freedom means the ability to make choices and freedom to be your best means nothing unless you are willing to do your best therefore you can choose to be your best or your worst, ultimately the decision is yours. Do not forget that, you are an original and there is no one exactly like you. Education on the other side, is not the filling of a part but the lighting of fire, because when you learn new ideas then fantastic new possibilities open to you.

Chapter 14

THE SECRET OF SUCCESS LIES WITHIN US

Knowledge is said to be a person's first step to solve problems and create wonderful ways to benefit society.

Whatever you can do or dream, you can begin it because boldness has genius; power and magic in it. An obstacle on the other hand is something that stands in the way of success but thinking of always trying to do more brings the state of mind in which nothing seems impossible. I discovered that, there is more treasure in books than in all the Pirate's loot on Treasure Island. Best of all I and You can enjoy these riches every day.

Let us think about our dreams and what we need to do to make them happen, but we must not forget to enjoy the journey. Hold fast to dream, for if dreams die, life is a broken winged bird that cannot fly. A person is known by the company he or she keeps hence people attract friends when they are honest and do nice things for others without expecting anything in return. In order to have friends, one must first be one by talking to others about positive things because by so doing, you are helping them to think in a positive way hence it is said: “A candle loses nothing by lighting another.

My free advice to the people is to keep our faces to the Sunshine so that we cannot see the shadow. That simply means, if we find a problem or difficulty , we should look for a solution outside ourselves hence I wrote these for the people especially from Mzansi who are willing to believe in themselves; willing to face challenges in life; willing to take responsibilities for their actions and who are willing to be successful in life.

The Researchers say: “Most people only use two percent of their potential and they do not use ninety eight percent of their brain. They stated that, the potential of the average person is like a huge Ocean not sailed or a new Continent unexplored which is the world of possibilities waiting to be released and channelled toward some great good. An individual cannot copy what an unsuccessful people do and expect to be successful but if a person chooses not to listen and not to work, he or she cannot be a success. The secret of success lies within us, starting with our thoughts which are followed by our actions and efforts that lead us to reaching our potential, just like a seed has power to ultimately become something greater. We have the same of future growth within us. What we see depends mainly on what we are looking for hence I accept failure, but I cannot accept not trying and for that I am prepared and hope that someday my chance will come.

Winston Churchill once said: "A Pessimist sees the difficulty in every opportunity whilst an Optimist sees that opportunity in every difficulty." This made me realise that, too many people tell themselves negative things all day long. They think they will not get good grades, or they will not win. This is a mistake because if you tell yourself that you cannot do something, your brain believes it.

I am a sacked teacher, and my limelight was taken away from me due to the rumour that had spiralled out of control because some people preferred to delude themselves than facing the truth. This became a wake - up call like icy water being poured over my head and I had to hit back or die hence certain issues were dropped. By whose instructions? Well currently I do not know.

It will be totally wrong for me to abandon my Principles of conciliation, tolerance and understanding hence I am not persuaded by provocation and anger to achieve anything because for me, conciliation is not about doing nothing but it is proactive; positive and hard work therefore I have to get between them to prevent confrontation and not to look idly while confrontation is happening.

Am I like a school of tiny, glittering fish hither and thither? Adversity brings out the best in people hence eye for an eye, a tooth for a tooth and fear for fear. It is better to fight to the bitter end than let them think I was easy even if it can be all shots in the dark. I discovered that, there are many flaws in my so-called 'case" hence I have decided to take the problem head on whilst they are still digging a bigger hole for themselves even if the cards are stacked against me.

I am a great believer in sinners being brought to book on the day of Judgement and that can only happen after the battle between good and evil. People like them who keep telling themselves that, they are going to be saved because they assume to have booked their places among the Righteous. I keep telling them that they are living in cloud cuckoo land because it is the nature of religion in which we are all damned that leads us to worship every god to be sure of a place in Heaven but they won't believe it.

In my research I learnt that Nero committed incest with his mother that he might be a second Oedipus and later he assassinated her so that he might realise the sensation of Orestes. It is also said, the one god immediately known to man was thenceforth the Divus Caesar whose throne in the sky was waiting empty for him till his earthly exile was ended.

In our days, we respected our elders without questions, but things have moved on. We cannot demand it anymore, but we have got to earn. Life would be easy if we never did anything, we requested and listened to the Priests and confessed our sins and attended the Church.

There is something damned odd going on concerning my so-called "Case" and "Convictions", but I cannot get a handle on it at all. I know none of us want a brush with the law as a result a con artist has taken them for a ride and will have them clean the mess because the said "Complainant" still sucks her thumb at night because children become footballs in these situations . My God! I was just trying to tie up the loose ends, but they could not keep their hands down till the trouble passed.

The Magistrate and his Prosecutors including the Department of Education Officials handled my so-called "Case" as if I were a Paedophile who is a man who suffers from a psychosexual disorder which predisposes him to find adolescent girls or boys attractive of which was an area that they left unexplored.

They did not consider the fact that the mental torture of anticipation was a thousand times worse than the brief pain of reality. I could not imagine a future without my wife and my family. Did I lack imagination of being a breadwinner? This led me to have the fear that I might be bewitched or someone out there was willing to put me out of the game but I blotted it out to avoid panic overload as I was trembling from head to toe.

I together with my family were terrified out of our wits because we did not know how long a piece was of string. My confidence is currently very shallow, but I should not put myself down even though I am like trying to stop a running horse. The Questions that came up in my mind were: "Was my habit of submission so ingrained that I accepted everything without questions?" OR "Is it true that a man could be turned on by the backs of a girl or woman knees?"

I wonder if I got the wrong end of the stick hence it was a slap in my face because she is her mother's clone who needed to make a noise to feel brave. It came to my attention that she gave her dead arm and lashed her viciously with her tongue as a result her hope gave way to fear and the terror of anticipation created a more powerful memory than the reality.

These deeds and accusations have often resulted in heavy compensation for miscarriages of Justice when alleged Villains proved to be innocent and the hunch was based on nothing more than a series of unfortunate coincidences. With what I have written, I think it is enough to make the Rozzers to sit up and think and stop listening with only half an ear because the said "Victim" had translated ideas into action.

All these happened to me as a result of a Cipher who is an Official without authority and the parent who insisted on the prosecution because she wanted someone to blame and to generate money just for her ill - mannered and disrespectful daughter hence the Magistrate decided to make an example of me . Well this is a common story.

My so-called “Case” needed real Police and Not a namby-pamby creature who fears his or her own shadows and who locks him or herself in and wait for the trouble to pass. I was put in the Nick because the so-called “Victim” is soothing her fears and instilling trust among herself and her small army.

In Prison I have learnt to cut people out of my head and put books and sports in their place because people who put me there are both dangerously egocentric. The first one is an Extrovert seeking her pleasure outside and the other is an Introvert seeking his pleasure inside, which suggests neither of them are seeing me as a person but merely to an end.

To one I may be an object of desire and to the other I may simply be the hostage that keeps them safe. Perhaps one sees me in both guises and perhaps both do because they used a child as their bait. They know that a frightened child is always an easy mark as they needed to be the centre of attention and if not, they make life for other people hell.

I do not approve men hitting women, not even the policewomen especially by tying them up and beat them black and blue. Some men use them as their work surface by making surreptitious deals with them because a deal is only a deal when it is honoured.

I could put money on the fact that the rich and the good-looking men are really sweet at the beginning until they get inside their knickers and find them no more exciting than the last girl or woman they had. Such men are only blind when it suits their convenience.

We live in a puritanical Society that refuse to acknowledge that children have sexual feelings. No court today would dare accept that a child could be a Seducer despite the statistical evidence that shows – Ebumnandini has the highest number of teenage pregnancies in the continent if not the world hence our government provides a child grant of which I believe that it is our country only which provides such a grant instead of providing the unemployed with unemployment grant until the unemployed get employment as other countries do.

Our government's corrupt law is against something which has been going on for centuries by an arbitrary laws putting ages on when it is legal to indulge which don't make a blind bit of difference because people are indirectly encouraged and allowed to persuade and not to coerce hence fear is a powerful emotion.

It came to my realisation that some people hide their heads in the sand and hope the problem goes away because once secrets are out then they lose their shame.

As a result they put me behind bars , innocent as I am, where I became a Samaritan because I used to sit for hours , helping my fellow inmates especially students that I was teaching by listening to their problems because I understood and still understand internalised fear and pain better than most as we were all in a place where ill health is endemic, potentially among both the young and the old inmates for whom the cold, wet conditions coupled with poor diets weakened them in totality and depression is common due to addiction to prescription pills.

I am a level-headed man, but I have got quite a temper when I am roused. I cannot see myself giving in easily because I was brought up in a culture where the dominant male sets the rules of behaviour within the family. Currently I am trapped against the wall; unable to advance; unable to retreat because as for me, such bastards need to be castrated for using our daughters and their mothers to push forth their hidden agendas especially by stringing their dicks in their mouths because such perverts ought to feel pain when they die.

CHAPTER 15

LET SLEEPING DOGS LIE

The question that always clicks my mind, "Is awareness more about where you are than who you are?" OR "Do you need to be sure; you are safe before you could acknowledge anything else? I believe in you scratching my back then I will scratch yours just like friendship calling.

Let me tell you a story about the Scorpion and the Frog.

The scorpion wants to cross a river, but he cannot swim, he then begs a ride from a frog. The frog begins by refusing because he is afraid the scorpion will sting him. The scorpion laughs and says he is not that stupid. "*If I sting you, you'll die, which means I will die too, because I can't swim.*" He tells the frog.

This persuades the Frog to do as the Scorpion asks, but halfway across the river the Scorpion sting him anyway

"Why did you do it?" asks the Frog as he is dying.
"*I could not help myself*" says the Scorpion, *"It is my nature."*
This story made me realise that a person can sometimes be in the wrong place at the wrong time hence we must start trying to help ourselves as it happened to me below the belt because someone is running a show with cowardice strategy but if you are loved, there'll always be a place where you are welcome.

In my point of view, to be born undistinguished is a less misfortune than to live hence wealth had no attraction for me even though I know that it is no light thing which I am undertaking.

I had sworn to defend myself and my family. I would rather die than betray my children hence I have decided that if the thieves take my belongings and clothes from me. I can walk and walk and walk the lighter like the lion which is tamed for a moment. Oh Yes! I may be dropsical for all that I know, but I will not be the water for them to swallow.
If they tie me fast and I could not help myself, I put my trust in the living rock in Heaven, the Lord - Jesus Christ and anchor my hopes in Him. He will direct me as a result they are going into unending torture. The hour will come when it will be having been too late for them. By Holy Name, we should be worse off if we are not allowed to die at all.

All Religious dogmatic systems are not content with insisting that there is high probability in their favour because they call themselves infallible. They demand on our part an absolute certainty that they are right although they disagree among themselves and cannot be all right. They tell us that doubtful is a sin and that we ought to be entirely certain. The difficulty is in the subject rather than in the treatment.

In my research I discovered that, seven and twelve are mystical numbers recurring continually in all legendary histories hence it is said, there are two kinds of Truths which are the truth of Facts which require a man of Science and the modern Historian, and the truth of Nature and Idea which require or demand the Poet and the Painter.

Some people cared nothing for useful knowledge, on the contrary they looked to be excited and amused which has resulted me to believe that, submission completes an entire unresolved resignation of our moral and spiritual intelligence for instance, believing in the Pope would soon lead people to believe in Jupiter.

It is said, Science thrives in the sunlight because able men are engaged upon different Departments of knowledge. They are all dependent on one another for instance the Geologists; the Physiologists and the Chemistry require the help of each other. The Astronomers cannot stir without the Mathematician and the Telescope Maker, which clearly indicates that, not a single branch of enquiry can be pursued successfully alone.

It is better to be noble in morals than to be noble in blood. I like to taste my friends but not to eat them and I do not consort with people whom I despises. On the other hand, I do not despite people who show me a thousand kindness. I can assure you with no shame that my zest for my work was terrific, but some people intends to turn me to ridicule and converts me into ten times the vicious old devil I already am.

I have much work upon my hands as I was a shining light of which the children; parents and the world must not be deprived hence my fear abated. I anticipated nothing about all these allegations against me because my conscience is clear hence, I left my seniors to decide based on my work record as well as my experience.

The so-called terrible Principal or Manager or Employer that the Department of Education has brought among our mist in our School was behind all my misfortunes. The Question which is bothering me in my mind is: "If this Person is so powerful with his persuasions, what will he do if he tries force?"

We must therefore be careful not to drive him to extremities even though I have already done by challenging him with his surreptitious dealings with the so said "Complainants" and become a major role player on the matters that do not concern him.

The other Questions which came in my mind were:" Why allegations against me were discussed in under cover of darkness?" and "Are the so-called "Complainants" ready to name and shame the real abuser? "What happened to me made me realise that the most ridiculous rumours spread like wildfire.

Let me try and open your minds of what happened when it all started. First I was called in the Principal's Office without been informed about such a meeting or should I say hearing and without my knowledge of anything wrong because he knew I was desperate to cling to the only thing that gives me life - meaning my job hence he axed me like a woodland and replaced with concrete.

He as a responsible person for setting the Agenda and convening such meetings or hearings but he convened that meeting or hearing informally without anyone's knowledge including myself and in the absentia of SGB members as well as my Union representative – SADTU. He even overruled one of his chosen SMT (School Management Team) member who wanted the issue raised and discussed.

Have I jeopardized my pensions? The answer is a big NO because I prefer to let sleeping dogs lie because I believe soon those responsible for my temporary or permanent downfall will weep crocodile tears because Teachers who genuinely care for children get crucified for leaving children with someone so inadequate.

I failed to defend myself as a result of irresponsible and greedy Attorneys and SADTU representatives for being easily convinced and maybe bribed to let my so-called "Case" go without any concrete or circumstantial evidence as well as with the wrong procedures that were followed from start to an end.
My so-called "Enemies" as they have turned up to be have also failed by not getting what they actually wanted from me which is R180 000 as a blackmail for the crime that does not exist as well as for jealousy of my success.

So, my failure helped me to change direction to be more successful than before and to prove them wrong for their evil deeds. I do not define myself as a failure because for me, Failure is a process and not identity. By accepting the situation in which I find myself gives me a good opportunity to make better choices in future and I fully agree that success is easy to handle as I did but handling failure takes courage.

Failure gave me an opportunity to grow to the point where I can handle things and challenges that lay ahead of me. Oh Yes! I regard the fact that, the glory is never in falling but it is in rising every time I fall hence I realised that my so-called "Enemies" wanted what they can't have and have what they don't want, for that reason a thorough investigation needs to be done as they have almost made a beggar of me . Well, if I am wrong, I am wrong.

I have decided to eat and drink for tomorrow because I am tossed on an Ocean of vain hopes and vain regrets. Thanks to my Almighty Father Who art in Heaven for giving me an opportunity to live in perfect simplicity and unbroken health of mind and body as a result of one intelligible sentence containing truth in it, is better than a hundred in an unknown tongue.

Some people have no mercy on their own bodies and non on others. Such people who inhabit these rocks are hard as the rocks themselves. I hope that, their clothes will scrape the flesh from their bones and that discipline will tear their bones out of such frail limbs as theirs. I believe, with the good will of all Parties including myself and no wrong done to any person then the first obstacle would have been overcome but they counted money lost which they'll spend on their soul's health. I therefore let them keep it since they love it so dearly or rather, they cannot keep it, for they must die and let it go to others who will not thank them.

An Angel from above will appear to enter their houses as a Spectator of the conflict. They will spring to Him; clutch Him and wrestle like Jacob with Him to extort a blessing but could not succeed and at last they will sink exhausted on the ground. I therefore regard a noble family only as an honourable setting for a nature which is noble.

What I experienced is like a story of a 100 years old man who after his complain and dissatisfaction concerning their Church Bishop's greediness and jealousy in comparison with other Churches as a result he was ordered in the midst of a bitter winter to repair an old Church far away. He shrank from the journey and begged to be spared. When the command was persisted in, he refused obedience therefore he was instantly expelled, half-clad amidst the ice and snow.

He wandered from one religious house to another. In all, he was refused admission. At last, one bitter frosty night he appeared penitent at the gate of the Church and prepared to be forgiven.

The Gatekeeper was forbidden to open to him till morning and left the old man to shiver in the snow through the darkness. The next day, when the gates were opened for him, the old man said: *"Had you been a bean last night between my teeth, they would have chopped you in pieces in spite of me."*

These stories taught me that, a person knows not what mercy means. We therefore find ourselves in the hands of Writers who themselves saw what they describe and who knew as well as we know the distinction between truth and falsehood and who could notice and appreciate genuine human qualities.

We Ebumnandinans especially us "Blacks" are the nation of more than fifty million but inferior in mental and physical capabilities to no other people in the world. In my research I have discovered that, the English are instinctively brave and noble - minded because to them, the Traditions of the past are powerful and men will fight for their homes because without a home they and their families are turned shelter less adrift for instance if he is thriving himself, his family is broken up and their house will become a pigsty.

For the English, the idea of home is inseparably connected with the possession or permanent occupation of land where a man's property is in money and a slip of paper will transfer it to any part of the world to which he pleases to send it. Where it is in the skill of his hands, there is another hemisphere open to him and where Employers speaking his own language are eager to secure his services.

Chapter 16

WE ARE WHAT WE EXPECT

I realised that a family which occupied a place for one or two years, will leave it without difficulty but to remove tenants after a half dozen generations is like tearing up a grown up tree by the roots of which will result for inadequate people to dominate thus for me, life is not one way street hence criticism is corrosive and eating away at self - esteem and ravaging trust.

I think it is unwise in our country - Mzansi according to the principles on which ministers of the parliament are selected for their several posts and to trust them with larger powers than they possess because when their ministry is formed, the selection lies between peers of great territorial influence for whom places must be found as the price and not due to their qualifications or skills but because of their support to the Party and Politicians - remarkable for readiness of speech, debating power and dexterity in influencing divisions thus for me is like putting a junkie in charge of a drug store and as for me, men like them should be locked up for life.

If our Government cannot learn the lesson for itself, then nothing. I only want to mend fences but out of sight is out of mind hence for me is like looking for a needle in a blasted haystack even though Tomorrow is soon enough to resume negotiations.

How dare do they override my authority because I am responsible for the debts I incur therefore I put asterisk beside their names because the quid pro quo for all their evil deeds is that they should never expect me to bail them out of a problem again. It is a clear - cut choice.

Litigation had crippled my fortune and the famine finished it even though the fortunes of the possessors of the soil of any country are bound up in the fortunes of the country to which they belong and such nations have always been the most stable in which the land is most widely divided and where the largest number of people have a personal concern in it.

We cannot escape from our nature because interest and natural feeling coincide to produce the same result. The world is not outgrowing associations of this kind and it never will outgrow them because attachment to locality is part of the human Constitution.

I could only interpret what I saw from what I thought I knew as I am currently pinned like a butterfly to a board; unable to break free but I sowed a seed of hope for the future hence I feel as if a weight had dropped from my shoulders . What I have penned down is taken from real life, not from fiction.

We prayed; we flogged; we fasted, and we confessed; still, Satan can buffet us. I have no fear for my soul, and I think my body will die in struggle because I cannot take the steam out of everything.

Do not just each day by the harvest you reap but by the seed you plant because the secret of your future is hidden in your daily routine. Yes! Everything is hard before it is easy therefore you should be ready to fail every time you try something. Remember! Failure brings you closer to your next success. For that reason, try your best to overcome all the challenges you face.

People are not remembered by how few times they fail but by how often they succeed. People know you by things you have done, not by the things you thought about doing. Henry Ford once said: "Mistakes move you closer to success." So, do not do less than you are asked but challenge yourself to do more because lots of effort will always bring you lots of success and then become what you think about.

No matter how discouraged you become, never let a failure or a problem stop you. Never leave till Tomorrow what you can do today because people who are honest are trustworthy and dependable. People who always try new things have a better chance at being truly successful even though they may not be successful the first time hence it is said: "An opportunity follows struggle, then follows effort and then follows hard work and it does not come before."

It is said, when an Archer misses the mark, he turns and looks for the fault within himself. Failure to hit the bull - eye is never the fault of the target or a bow. Therefore, to improve your aim, improve yourself. You can also make greater improvements toward your goals by taking responsibility for your own weaknesses by working through those areas.

An Archer do not blame anyone else for missing the Centre of the target instead he thinks about his technique and how much more practice may be needed. At the end he is responsible for his level of improvement. If a person wants to be a better Athlete; a better Reader; a better Friend and so on, he or she must identify the barriers to his or her success.

Each day is said to be the building block that leads a person to future success and greater challenges. When sailing, a person can encounter all sorts of obstacles such as dangerous changes in the way of our goals hence some people have thousands of reasons why they cannot do what they want to. When all they need is one reason of why they can. The crucial thing to remember is to take action that moves you in the direction of your goal even when obstacles arise.

One of the secrets of success is to refuse to let temporary setbacks defeat us. In my research I discovered that, Henry Ford whilst developing

Automobiles, people told him that he was wasting his time. In fact, he failed and ran out of money for his project five times before he was successful, but he kept going. Look! How many cars are on the roads these days? This confirms what was once said by Robert F Kennedy:" Only those who dare to fail greatly can ever achieve greatly."

Everyone who wants to do amazing things need to believe that he or she can do it. Remember! We are what we expect. Let us therefore not think that, great success is impossible just because we are not great at everything. In my research I have also discovered that, Whoopi Goldberg had a learning disability that made her Schoolwork difficult and that Tom Cruise had a really bad time with reading. Look! Both can do amazing things with their lives.

Mark Twain once said:" Positive friendship help you become great ." meaning that we should keep away from people who try to belittle our ambitions because small opportunities lead to great accomplishments and for that reason , we should try new things . Anyone who refuses to learn new things, robs him or herself of an exciting rich life because opportunities are everywhere hence we must always let our hooks hanging because when we least expect it, a great fish will swim by.

In each of us, there is a seed. A seed of vast potential; a tiny seed needs to be planted and cared for , before it can become a wonderful strong tree thus a seed is only the beginning of an amazing journey that involves change and transformation . Fear on the other hand, makes it easy to worry about problems and it can also make it easy to avoid doing something about problem. It is true! Action conquers fear but we need to be prepared first because preparation requires effort and determination.

A life spent making mistakes is not only more honourable but more useful than a life spent doing nothing. Time on the other side is something a person can never get back if we waste it. Spending time, thinking about the past rather than tuning in to what is important presently, is a mistake. It is just like regretting the friends we have lost, will not help us make new friends anytime soon because he or she who spends time regretting the past, loses the present and risks the future.

I personally have no talent, but I am merely extremely inquisitive hence I realised that, by telling the truth can save us from having to tell more lies. Patient people do not do things out of anger or haste, but they take their time to think about why things are happening around them? Therefore, patience will keep them from making mistakes.

We live in times of change that is Political change; Intellectual change and change of all kinds. Opinions will or must be disturbed from time to time because things are changing and have to change but they change very slowly. We must therefore make up our minds to be poor by caring only for what is true and right and good. On these conditions, we may add something real into the Intellectual stock of mankind and mankind in return may perhaps give us bread enough to live upon even if the bread is extremely thinly spread with butter.

Times have changed but we are still surrounded by temptations and they are no longer appear in the shape of stake and gallows. They come rather as Intellectual perplexities on the largest and gravest questions which concerns us as human creatures. Perplexities with regard to which self - interest is perpetually tempting us to be false to our real convictions. The best that we can do for one another is to exchange our thoughts freely.

The fact of growing older teaches many of us to respect notions which we once believed to be antiquated a few more years of life, whether years bring wisdom or do not bring it, is far from certain. I will follow the train of my thought which suggests our presence at this place and the purpose which brings us here. I presume that almost all of us intend to belong. If we mean to thrive then we must take one line , rigidly and sternly confine our energies on it hence I strongly believe that No human beings are machines that are doing good work conscientiously and honestly with the fear of our Maker before us .

Of all evil spirit in our so-called "Democratic Ebumnandini" at this hour in the Continent, Insincerity is the most dangerous. I therefore suggest that we be honest with ourselves with whatever temptation; say nothing to others that we do not think and play no tricks with our own minds because the Eternal truths and rights of things do exist.

Fortunately, we have independent of our thoughts and wishes, therefore no one shall make me profess to think true what I believe to be false and no one shall make me do what I do not think to be just. I believe other people have a good a right to their opinions as we have to ours.

We cannot make true things false or false things true by choosing to think so and we cannot vote right into wrong or wrong into right. I suggest that, we must assert our own freedom if we must or should, but we must assert it with modesty and quietly by respecting others as we wish to be respected ourselves. Above all, to our own selves be true and the rest will follow as the night to the day, for that we cannot be false to any person.

I believe, no one can thrive upon denials hence positive truth of some kind is essential as food both for mind and character. Every child born into the world should be put in the way of maintaining his or herself in an honest independence and go out into the world with the knowledge as there are a great many good things in it of which it will be highly pleasant to get hold of.

I discovered that the child that is kindly nurtured; wisely taught and assisted to make his or her ways in life does not depend on his or her parents but he or she is proud of his or her family and jealous for the honour of the name he or she bears. A poor man's child on the other hand is brought here with no will of his or her own. We therefore have no right to condemn him or her to be a rogue because he or she may fairly demand to be put in the way of earning his or her bread by labour hence a tree must be rooted in the soil before it can bear flowers and fruits.

We must learn to stand upright upon our feet; to respect ourselves and to be independent of charity or accident. I discovered in my research that, there are but three ways of living which are by working; by begging and by stealing. Ultimately those who do not work are begging or stealing.

Is it okay if we take no thought of what we shall eat or what we shall drink or with what we shall be clothed and take for granted that, our Heavenly Father knows that we have a need of these things?

CHAPTER 17

WHAT WAS ONCE AN ENTHRALLING GAME IS NOW A DEADLY BORE

It is clearly stated that, a person is not considered entitled to live if he or she could not keep him or herself from starving.

I learnt that, when we begin in our work in this world, we value most than the approbation of those older than ourselves. As we advance in life, we learn the limits of our abilities hence our expectations for the future shrink to modest dimensions and the question with us is no longer what we shall do but what we have done. We call ourselves to account for the time and talents which we have used or misused. It is then that the good opinion of those who are coming after us becomes so peculiarly agreeable.

If we have been roughly handled by our contemporaries, it flatters our self - conceit to have interested another generation. For that reason, I shall not depart an outcry of this life till my tongue glorify His Name on this earth because we ourselves are made of earth and our work is on this earth hence we are common place people who are obliged to make the most of our time.

A person is like a clay in the Potter's hand of which one vessel is made to honour and another to dishonour and the idea only is immortal and never fades hence the world is to be let alone in its pleasures. Its sins of which the church relegated to opinion with free liberty to split doctrinal hairs to the end of time which has resulted to the visible product of material civilisation where there is No fear of God in the middle of it.

Isn't Spirit more than matter? Is there no such thing as pure intellectual culture?

I learnt that; philosophy will bake no bread, but it gives us our souls. It gives us heaven and it gives us knowledge of those grand truths which concern us being immortal being. These days, churches have been double, theological books, reviews, magazines, newspapers, and many others have poured out by hundreds of thousands. By the side of it, there has sprung upon equally astonishing development of moral dishonesty hence I no longer trust that any article that I buy is the thing which it pretends to be.

I have never in my life during all my past wonderful and sometimes painful

Years of living on this earth did I ever come across among all the Religious people, it could be Preachers; Pastors; Deacons; Bishops and so on. On verbal inspiration, never one that I recollect on common, honest to the primitive Commandment: "Though shalt not lie; though shalt not steal."

The Poet - Coleridge once said: "Every man might have two versions of his or her Bible of which one is the book that he or she reads and the other is the trade that he or she pursues, where he or she will find perpetual illustrations of every Bible truth in the thoughts which his or her occupation might open to him or her."

We have nowadays false weights; false measures; cheating and shoddy everywhere hence the Commercial life of our country - Ebumnandini has been saturated with fraud and so deep has it gone that a strictly honest Tradesman can hardly hold his or her ground against competition.

The established Authorities are in possession of the field and are naturally desirous to keep it. There is no kind of service which they more eagerly reward than the support of clever fellows who have dipped over the edge of latitudinarianism, who profess to have sounded the disturbing currents of intellectual seas and discovered that they are accidental or unimportant.

Now we are reaping the reward of our carelessness because we have raised up against ourselves just for a mighty Empire to be rival so that it may be the successful rival of our power. We sent foreign countries like for example America our skilled labourers and had offered them a home in the enormous territories that belong to us especially "Chinese" instead of sending them to places where they would have been no burden but a blessing which could have resulted in injustice and heedlessness bearing proper fruits.

I discovered that, every honest occupation to which a person sets his or her hand would raise him or her into a Philosopher if he or she masters all the knowledge that belong to his or her craft . Every occupation even the meanest but productive, if followed assiduously with a desire to understand everything connected with it will be an ascending stair whose summit is nowhere and from which the successive steps of which the horizon of knowledge perpetually enlarges.

I have realised that, each step of knowledge gained in the things that a worker even the poor can be immediately applied and realised for instance, Each point of Science which the Labourer masters will make him or her not only a wiser person but a better workman, and will either lift him or her if he or she is ambitious to a higher position or make him or her more intelligent and more valuable if he or she remains where he or she is.

A person's work become more profitable while he or she become wiser which he or she may go for or he or she may stop short. Whatever he or she does and what he or she has assigned will be real gain and become part and parcel of him or herself.

In my research I discovered that the world requires handicraft, and that soil requires those whose work is with the brain or with the brain and hand combined like Doctors; Lawyers; Teachers; Engineers and so on. It is on this basis only that any superstructure of intellectual cultivation worth having can be possibly be built hence for me the Ten Commandments and a handicraft still makes a good and wholesome equipment to commence life with.

A really great person has to create the taste with which he or she is to be enjoyed because there are splendid exceptions of merit, eagerly recognised and early rewarded. Your success as well as mine will vary as the goodness of our work better for ourselves; conscious for our Souls and for the world we live in. People who cannot, are likely to be exasperated into unwise demonstrativeness; to become in Politics;

radicals in thought and their private disapprobation bursts into open enmity. If they continue upon this road, it leads them to no healthy conclusions.

Times have changed as a result an Apprentice plan has broken down, partly because it is abused for purpose of Tyranny; partly because Employers do not care to be burdened with Employees whose labour is unprofitable; partly because it opens no road for exceptional clever person or Employee to rise into higher positions because Employees are started in a groove from which they could never afterwards escape. The original necessities on the other hand remain unchanged; practical ability and the Ten Commandments are obligatory as ever.

Wordsworth clearly stated in his Poem that, ours is but sleep and forgetting. The soil that rises with us - our life's star hath elsewhere had its settings and cometh from afar; not in entire forgetfulness and not in utter nakedness, but trailing clouds of glory do we come, from Heaven, which is our home.

God! For three or more years and nine Months, I have been unable to handle my so-called "Case" of the so-called "Unnatural Sexual Offence "or whatever they called it. Please, let me turn it over to you. After praying, immediately a great feeling of peace descended upon me, intermingled with a feeling of being suffused with a quiet strength.

I then realised that , Esibayeni is the place I have to return to , not only because I must face the mess I have found myself into or made there , but because it was there that I could be the most service in such unfair and fabricated cases . I have something to contribute to humanity since I am peculiarly qualified and a fellow - sufferer, to give Aid and comfort to those who have stumbled and fallen over this business of meeting life hence I feel myself as useful member of the human race at last.

There is no fool like an old fool. I regard people who are foolish in old age as very foolish people who live in glass houses and they should not throw stones. Why one loses on the swings one makes up on the round abouts. Can there be excitement in a Card game played eternally with both Players for ever holding the same Cards? There cannot , just like any girl or woman , if the body she possess is not actually deformed and the face badly moth - bitten BUT she is still going to become acquainted with the gentle art of seduction fairly early in life hence it is said : What was once an enthralling game is now a deadly bore."

I believe that , The latest part of my life has a purpose not in great things accomplished but in daily living hence things had just gone from bad to worse , meaning that , I had to give up a lot of the things that I had been accustomed to . That was not the easiest thing in the world for me and my family as I have my ups and downs, the same as the rest. People tell tales out of School so as to swim with the tide and they look through rose coloured spectacles as I served time by suffering imprisonment because some people took advantage of my good nature by fabricating and inventing with evil motive thus I had to stand on the edge of a volcano which is an indication of coming disaster hence the writing on the wall.

Currently I am facing a stone wall to be above water as I am in low water, as much water has flowed under the bridge but I believe every cloud has a silver lining and that fortune favours the brave even though the care on the other hand killed the cat. I strongly believe that if one has been evil in speech or act, one generally suffers for it thus chicken come home to roost. I therefore prefer not to talk too much because it is said: "Speech is silver, and Silence is golden. I believe that one swallow does not make a summer and that one good turn deserves another. It came to my realisation that people of the same occupation often quarrel as each thinks he or she knows best hence it is said: "Two of a trade never agree " therefore to win success, one must take risks. If one is careful in small things, there will be less difficulty in the bigger ones. I am trying to fish in troubled waters as I am in the teeth of a Gale, but I hope it will blow over.

There was a bull in a China Shop who looked as if butter would not melt in his or her mouth. I am not drawing a long bow because I know we are in the same box. I had to undertake responsibility at short notice as I locked the stable when the horse was already stolen by backing the wrong horse and this became a hue and cry. I had to kiss the rod meaning I had to submit to punishment meekly without complaint as I was an underdog with no one to help a lame dog over a stile because I was at a loose end.

The trouble was caused by an unintentional or mischievous word or deed and I had to get more kicks than half pence and they then strained at a gnat and swallowed a camel to cook my goose. At the eleventh hour, I realised that I should have struck while the iron was still hot by breaking the ice but instead, I acted out of labour of love. Unfortunately, we could not see eye to eye with them hence I rode for a fall by taking it lying down.

I learnt that the first small move is likely to lead to more serious changes hence it is said: "The thin end of the wedge "but this for me is just all my eye and Betty Martin, meaning "Nonsense." They made a mountain out of a mole hill so as to throw mud at me hence they caught me napping as if I am having a bad reputation and this became a rough passage for me and became the swig of the pendulum.

I had to keep stiff upper lip and believe that they will be caught in their own trap because, money burns a hole in the pocket especially hush - money which is a bribe. All these has come to light that in future I had to toe the line or mark instead of crying for the moon because there are people who have a rod in pickle for me and forced me to eat humble pie. They play off one person against another to dig a pit for me and to queer my pitch by putting difficulties in my way intentionally. What am I to do to clear the pitch?

CHAPTER 18

WHAT ARE THEY? ROBOTS!

Presently I have not a shirt to my back which is the root of the matter as I do not know where the shoe pinches so as to deal or reckon with and to serve one right as a broken reed with a hang dog look. Nothing like the unexpected for keeping people on their toes hence I believe it is worse for them than it is for me. No sensible person would ever want to meet people like them.

I would have to keep my memory green because there are wolves in sheep's clothing. They have pulled wool over my eyes with a Judas kiss so as to drop the pilot all because of a Poohbah who is a pompous and important person who claims to be the master of most things and a Paul pry or a meddling fellow hence I met my waterloo or suffered decisive defeat.

I believe, actions are better than words hence still waters run deep - meaning that silent people often possess surprising powers of thought and action. It is clearly stated that, Determination usually find a way to success and that we often believe what we most want to believe thus "The wish is father to the thought." It is also said, people of similar character are usually found together thus an adage: "Birds of a feather flock together."

Once bitten, twice shy therefore I had to mend my ways because some people raise false alarm. I learnt that, men are masters of their fate - meaning that every man is the Architect of his own fortune so as to be the apple of one's eye instead of being up in arms hence I did not swallow the bait even though I was put between Scylla and Charybdis - meaning between two difficulties which were Labour and Criminal issues due to draconian policies and told it in Gath by the descendants of Ananias.

Being a hail – fellow. Well met and fit as a fiddle. Let my pride and anger stop me as a matter of life and death to bring to light in dribs and drabs that the man who can keep order can rule the world. I believe good Departments are the sign of an orderly mind. I shall find out all about them in due course as the whole School and the Community is raving mad as a result I dislike argument because for me it serves no useful purpose and I cannot endure disorder thus idle chatter for me is also an inefficient waste of energy . No one else's reports are of any use to me because their eyes hidden, and their expressions are unreadable.

I would have to be careful or something nasty would happen. I should learn not to be disorganised. I realised that, if one goes on nosing, one will get into trouble. I have worked out a good system for having a quiet life and I do not want anyone interfering with it. People must wait and see. I just wish I did look like a demon that might frighten them away as they are breathing down my neck even though I avoided them even harder than they avoided me. What are they? Robots! Or who is the man at the wheel? Am I daydreaming?

It is clearly stated that, fine feathers make fine birds. All is not gold that glitters. *OH – HE! Ukhala ngani*? *Amakati akhala ngobisi*! East, West, home's best. I am not the person who goes with the stream to make a clean breast of what happened in order to save one's breath to cool one's porridge even if wheels within wheels instead of whitewashing me as a person.

Brag is a good dog, but Holdfast is a better as a steppingstone for a tower of strength to be a cornerstone in the Community. Tête-à-tête with those sitting on the fence. I told them that he who laughs best is the one who laughs last because what I experienced in my life is a long lane that has no turning. Therefore, I should live and let live because the mill will not grind with the water that has already passed.

My experience taught me that, money makes the mare go and at the same time money is the root of all evil. I also learnt that a watched pot never boils as a result pride goes before a fall thus the proof of the pudding is in the eating. I discovered that, a rolling stone gathers no moss and that even walls have ears and that the little pitchers on the other hand have big ears.

I don't want to beat about the bush as I was put in a tight corner so as to lose the day by using Fabian tactics in my so-called "Cases" so that I could take a French leave or use Billingsgate language but I am not a Dunce for a Siren and Punic faith so as to cause their sardonic laughter . Maybe they thought I am in the arms of Morpheus or I'll bury myself, forgetting that I am kind and generous without a thought of immediate gratitude or return and that I don't feel blue easily. All I do or say, I do or say a thing without hesitation hence "To make no bones about a matter at hand."

Maybe I have had an unnatural upbringing hence I am the unusual guy who in spite of my kindness and my generosity, there was something which repelled them. She was obedient to her mother only because she feared her as a result, she could sulk for days. She was at the root of my depression and it was necessary to rid my mind of this absurd notion. Facing the abominable truth, I was unprepared to find myself confronting such a highly finished piece of nature and we ended evenly matched. How was I to know I was going to meet her as she had?

Remember I have lived amongst soldiers and I seem to have thrown off the blue devils as a result sleep for me was far away as ever because pride had become an obsession. My wife on the other hand is our good

Angel, a ray of sunshine in the house hence we fell head over ears in love with each other.

Currently I must remember that it is the fate of great men always to be misunderstood. They have underestimated my determination because people round here are not only mad but stupid as she was one of the headmaster's goody - goodies but I am invulnerable and can't be hypnotised. Why everyone was so well behaved? Well, I hate not understanding things for instance, the neat rows of learners formed and filed into School premises and that the LRC - Learner's Representative Council were the voice of the Head Master therefore they must be obeyed thenceforth Teachers and Learner's teeth clattered together uncontrollable due to fear.

The Headmaster took whatever actions as he or she saw fit without listening to other stake - holders. Surprisingly even in the Courts, people can have Lawyers to speak for them hence they are not to let me off whatever I say. "Be quiet!" a voice in my head was saying, "Because women's success is the backbone of the nation."

OH – YES! Fairness is an illusion which is designed to create disorder but the person who can endure disorder is truly free. I had put my hand to the plough and to die in harness as there is nothing to write home about neither here nor there. I don't know why my Headmaster was so bossy. "Just answer the question!" There was no friendliness in his voice because he held the trump card hence he was able to build castles in the air and gave them a blank cheque to trump up a charge against me hence I ended under a cloud whilst he himself was in clover. Should I hold their hands and tell them bedtime stories so that they could be out of my hair?

Maybe I was not fit to hold the candle to challenge the situation and to let the cat out of the bag but I still have a card up my sleeve to make capital out of as I am prepared to give chapter and verse of the whole incident as they are orange onions with silver skins . I should not have told her a thing and let her find it all out for herself because I tried to catch her eye, but she didn't see me. "Never be too clever, I should have known that." I thought. I should have slipped quickly out of the door before the Headmaster mouth a question at me as his motto was: "Please do not speak until you are asked!"

Maybe I am carrying coals to Newcastle hence a wild - goose chase which resulted to the cap and bells to Bystanders who were snooping around. All these led me began to munch my piece of cake whilst frowning over a difficult problem. People need not go thinking I am thick or anything and they should have the memory green as it is good for the Soul being startled, because most men are today hen - pecked to keep their heads above water otherwise "*Bazolinda ibhasi elingasoze lafika.*"

I have 100 children. 90% of them have sharp noses like me. 85% of them have bald like most men do. 80% of them have on leg and 75% are lisping.

How many bald; one-legged, lisping children with sharp noses must I have? My answer is 30 children.

Diamond cut diamond and the die is cast because it is on the horns of a dilemma but I am prepared to die in the last ditch to stand on my dignity and that would be a square deal between the devil and the deep blue Sea with no cock of the walk who will fabricate or invent a cock - and - bull story so as to pay someone back in his or her own coin, which is said to be, to give tit for tat because that will be to tread on someone's corn of which is a dead letter but the crack of doom is coming as currently it is a rainy day because the blind is leading the blind instead of weighing in the balance but that for me presently is like a blind alley.

I suggest that, all and sundry should deal away with the old Adam by pocketing an affront until the coast is clear to clear the air. I was taken aback as I thought I was beating the air on my own account without any assistance but for me, half a loaf is better than no bread because procrastination is the thief of time. I realised long ago that; an empty vessel makes the most sound hence I've decided to set a thief to catch a thief.

How can a Benedict tantalize a modern Amazon these days? It could lead to a malapropism with even an evidence of a Billet - doux as there will be no amende honourable in our justice and labour Departments except for an alibi. That for me is nowadays a chic - meaning "Stylish." Hence, I was out of the frying pan into the fire and that I am prepared to proclaim from the house - tops even if it rains cats and dogs.

People may believe me and accept my compliments as she is a creature of moods ; behaving like a child and for that , she must be treated like one unless she mends her ways hence we resembled nothing so much as two cats trying to stare one another out. What has happened to put them all on end?

What brought me back in town in such a crack? What happened to bring me in such a bang? Well! Beggars cannot be Choosers because currently I am poor as a Church rat, but life goes on. When I always about to retire in bed, the following question clicks in my mind: "Am I preaching long and very dull Sermons?"

It is clearly stated that, fortune favours fools and that forewarned is fir armed. Well! I hope so but I do not depend on it hence I will leave no stone unturned to weather the storm and to find out who casted the first stone on my family tree? Things are currently topsy - turvy due to a ticket - of - leave I received to wax and wane my chances of being employable again as I am not willing to go to the wall as I got wind off those who tries to throw cold water on me.

We must be ready to pay the price as good things will not just fall onto your lap without any hard work or preparation.

Have you ever heard that, one day God decided to shuffle animal kingdom? He started with Coloured and Indian people. "From now on, you shall become white!" Coloured and Indian people were beside themselves with excitement.

Next were the South African indigenous groups, the Nguni now became Coloured and they too rejoiced at God's mercy. Next up, the Sotho people who graduated to being Nguni. And so on. God elevated every group to occupy the space left by the South Africans considered superior to them. But conviviality came to a stop when God told the Monkeys that they could take over the status of Shangaans and Vendas, who made up the last group on thrung occupied by humans. The Monkeys baulked:" *Ungamane uyeke*" Meaning, you might as well leave it. They said in defiance of God's wishes.

CHAPTER 19

UTHINI-KE UMA SEKUNJENA? UMDALI UKHONA!

Correctional Services! Tell me!

What do you correct to Prisoners or Inmates?
If I am still having previous convictions as lifetime record.
And that Record will haunt me for the rest of my life.

I cannot find jobs as a man to feed and to take care of my children.
I am not accepted by the community as a changed person.

Why were we brought in prison?
Is it the profit that they earn by keeping prisoners in prisons?

Don't you see that you are instilling crime in our country?
This is no time for spreading propaganda. Only a fool who will agree with this foolishness. In prisons we are harassed on daily basis. The food we eat is not enough and not healthy. The hospital of Prison is like in hell.
The cells in which prisoners are locked are cold as an ice-cold refrigerator. No this is not a normal life for human beings, even the Prisoner's Unions are not functioning.

You build prisons instead of creating jobs for the unemployed citizens of this country.

UTHINI-KE UMA SEKUNJE?

Konke okushilo ukuba kwenzeke ngami,
Kwenzekile.
Ngenxa yamazwi omlomo wakho.
Yebo! Unginyathelile, wangiciphiza,

Ngoba bengimncinyane njengentuthwane.

Yebo! Izingubo namajazi owembetheyo,
Usenkundleni yokwahlulela – amnyama.
Enza ungezwa kodwa unezindlebe,
Awuboni kodwa unamehlo.
Okulungileyo kubi emehlweni akho.
Impela wayithengisa
Impilo yakho kusathane.
Wafunga nokufunga ukuthi
UYihlo noNyoko uzobafaka ejele.
Kungakanani-ke,
Mina ngingelutho kuwe?

Ngiyinja ekhonkothayo,
Ekhangwe ngeketango entanyeni.
Ngisendlini yobugqila.
Noma ngikhala, abaphathi bejele,
Bavala izindlebe zabo,
Ukuba bangezwa lutho,
Ngenxa kanembeza

Walowo ongenacala.

Umndeni wami uyaphela,
Ngisetilongweni,
Ngivalelwe,
Ngalahlekelwa nangumsebenzi,
Kodwa ngingenacala.
Mabajabule- ke labo,
Osizene nabo ukuba kugcine
Kwenzeke inhloso yabo; neyakho; kuze kubenje!

Uthi wazi amalungelo abantu?
Kodwa ngihlale ngihlukumezekile,
Imihla namalanga.

Kodwa uMvelingqangi,
USomandla, inkosi yamakhosi
Nophezu kwakho konke,
Akudalayo emhlabeni naseZulwini,
Uyakuzivula izindlebe Zakhe.

Ezwe ukukhala kwami nomndeni wasekhaya,
Ezimfihlakalweni, emangeni naseziluthweni
Kanye nasemoneni, nobusathane.

Yena uzongiphendulela ngisho khona,
Ukuthi uzongiphendula ngesikhathi Sakhe.

FOR MY BELOVED MOTHER

MAY HER SOUL REST IN PEACE

God has heard you,
But God answers when the time is right,
According to His Will.

Sometimes He answers quickly
Other times, we must wait for His answer.

Of course, He will sometimes tell us “NO”

We must learn to trust Him day by day
To answer our Prayers,
He will give us what we need.

AMEN

I love you. You are not "were" but still "are" the best Mother in the World and the best Teacher and the most important friend I could have.

TO MY FAMILY

God does not instantly deliver us from all our troubles
Instead He helps us develop character and strength
To walk through these problems.
As we trust God, we will have peace even
In the middle of difficulties like these.

It is now time to be strong and unite even in my absence.
I promise I will be with you soon,
God loves us just the way we are!

I learnt that, some black people are better than others, coloured people and Indians are better than black people and whites. How black people kept each other down. We as society are partly to blame for such attitude and behaviour because we hail being light as better and clearer than a darker skinned person hence skin lightening products.

Women who uses skin lotions to be light in complexion instead of being proud of their skin colour.

UMTHANDAZO WAMI WOKUCELA USIZO

Hamba nami Somandla, Nkulunkulu Baba,
Ebusuku obumnyama,
Nasekukhanyeni kwelanga.

Iba ngasohlangothini lwami,
Ubambe isandla sami
Ungihole endleleni engiyihambayo.

Kwesinye isikhathi le ndlela ibonakala iyinde,
Amandla ayangiphelela.
Manje, Mdali wami, ngicabanga Wena ukuze
Unginike amandla nomdlandla.
Amatshe avame ukungivalela indlela,
Ngiwe kwesinye isikhathi,
Kepha uhlale ukhona
Ukungisiza uma ngikumemeza.

Njengoba wathulisa umoya,
Wahamba phezu kolwandle,
Nqoba Mvelingqangi, Simakade Ophilayo,
Izivunguvungu ezingithusayo
Ezintabeni ezikhuphukelayo.

Njengoba welapha izishosha,
Wenza ukuba izimpumputhe zibone,
Ngisize uma ngiphelelwa ithemba,
Ngihambe ngiphakamisele ikhanda lami phezulu
Ngethembe Wena Wedwa, Mdali weZulu noMhlaba.

AMEN

In Season and out Season I climbed the rugged road to intellectual and cultural self - realisation. With horrible experience in my life I learnt that rumours fly and exaggerate with every telling because some people are more trouble than they are worth. I therefore told myself to overcome hardships and not be puffed up, to be in the throes of adversity and be unafraid; not to shrink from difficulties when they appear in the offing.

Disappointments and hardships followed each other's heels from the very start when informally invited in the presence of the so-called "Victim" and her mother with chosen few SMT members who were also informally invited and were not given a chance to air their views and worst of all in the absence of the SGB members .

Secondly when two Newspapers that is Uzalo News and Umphakathi News dated 19 - 20 October 2012 had breached Section 1.8 of the Code of Ethics and Conduct by publishing information about false allegations against me without first consulting me ; without my knowledge ; without hearing the side of my story and without my consent . The Press Code states that: "The Media shall seek the views of the subject of critical reportage in advance of publication", which they did not follow.

For me, the hottest place in hell is reserved for those who remain neutral in times of great moral conflict. How singular is life and how full of changes; how small a thing will ruin and save one thence I had some hard days since I saw them. I learnt that, beneath the surface of prosperity and peace is deep misery and bitter hatred hence the Rich becomes in time lazy and corrupt whilst the poor becomes spiritless and debased.

I think not that the darkness never ends because I believe when the day dawns, the Sun will greet me from the East. I would not in my life shower my enemies with favours before I could feel quite safe as there is no trace of unity among them. I know some people condemned me without even meeting me.

I am aware that I was pitied by some of my colleagues. Most of them have cosy homes and indulgent families. They go to parties; they are happy and have future while I am the victim of unscrupulous exploitation. Still I cannot make head or tail of all these accusations as a result they went from bad to worse, but I believe therefore great calamity will befall them.

The storm will not last forever, and when it has passed, a great calm will come. By then I will know that the time is ripe and turn over a new leaf.

Broken by difficulties, they thought I will grow rapidly aged and helpless, knowing we are back at the beginning again and that we shall never be able to plan such things again just as infidelity and blindness are likely to be answered by failure.

CHAPTER 20

CAUGHT IN THE CROSS FIRE

Have you ever heard of the story of ten frogs?

Well! It is said: Ten frogs decided to participate in a competition where they had to hop until they reach the top of a high mountain. The spectator frogs gathered around the mountain to watch the ten frogs competing to come out on to. All the spectators looked on with amazement as they believed that this was an impossible dream.

As the ten frogs started hopping, the crowd was cheering. The sceptical ones shouted, asking the ten frogs; "How they will do it? It has never been done before. Remember the others who died trying to hop to the top of that mountain? Just give up! You must accept that you are just frogs!" They yelled.

As the spectators continued shouting, the ten frogs started fainting and dying one - by one.

But one frog managed to reach the peak of the mountain. He won the Prize and proved all other frogs wrong.

When that frog was interviewed about how he made it to the top while others were fainting and dying?

He responded using the sign language and said:
"I am deaf so I could not hear what the other frogs were saying. I had to listen to my inner voice and just continue encouraging myself throughout the race."

It turned out that the only thing that killed the other nine frogs were negative voices of the Spectators.

They did not reach their destiny because they listened to destiny – delayers who never run out of negative words to say. So, they felt discouraged and died on the way.

For me to achieve anything that I set my mind on. I must be like that deaf frog and not pay attention to anything the "Naysayers" proclaim to me. I will just have to close my ears and embrace the courage and tenacity to climb the Mountain, No matter what.

Well! In my life, Hurdles came, that was when I knew how high I should jump and realised that, even it is hard, I should fight until the end. God will never forsake me. He knows my pain and He will heal me.

I've already known that the most limiting thing I can do is to compare myself to others by creating a better life for myself and my family while trying to keep up with others. This helps me to forget that life could be different on the other side of the fence.

Have you ever noticed that after passing through the valley of the shadow of death, just when you are enjoying the greener pastures, another shadow appears?

Life is a wonderful journey, and it is made up of a series of new beginnings hence Backstabbers are out to make me look incompetent and untrustworthy because they hope this will make them look better. This is often because they are insecure in their own jobs and lives as a result, they can be dangerous and malicious, pretending to be my best friends while they were and still are waiting for the perfect moment to pounce.

The man on top has zombified the entire leadership and no one can see anything wrong with him and I have to top up my game and match the standard but I have to close my eyes so that I don't see those who aim to discourage me, and close my ears to malicious talks.

I do not let any grass grow under my feet even if my future is at stake because I believe that all will be good. I will soon make it, it is not permanent, and it is a passing phase. Whatever situation I am in, I always remember and know that I am not alone and that God cares. My focus is not to give up because God is with me. I am courageous and knows that when the Lord is my Light and my Salvation, there is nothing to fear.

When the wicked advance against me to devour me, it is my enemies and my foes who will stumble and fall therefore I do no fear but walk tall and pursue my destiny.

How many twin Lesbians are out there who have seduced their mothers' boyfriends or peeping Toms who married their first cousins after spying them making love to their fathers? Will they be filing the reports for that? Maybe to them, it is not as bad as it sounds.

Maybe nothing would work because nothing was the matter hence I am doing what I do so that I can reclaim my future, and the only way I can do that, is by confronting my past . Today I had to answer the questions of the past before I could go on to the future.

My life has been an adventure and my adventures have resulted in my making enemies as well as friends. Things are not always what they seem. People never do anything without thinking it through well in advance. Such people have more money than brains and the kind who buried their frustrations and disappointments so deep.

I am not sure I know where to start as they had me eating out of the palms of their hands. Maybe the words pouring from my mouth are like boiling water from the kettle. I know good friends are hard to come by, but I believe and hope that there are people out there who might be willing to shed some light as these allegations and accusations has taken another little piece of my heart. These allegations and accusations against me will never be earthbound and forgotten by me or my family as they wish. This is WAR.

The rift between me and them is irreparable because some police can be tight - asses as one poor lost soul recognizing kindred spirit. In my life I have no extra - marital affairs. I am certainly not the paragon of the virtue people had heard eulogized these past years. Is there such a thing as an ex - wife - in - law for whom I am accused and acquitted for? Well, they are nuttier than a fruitcake.

If I could be given an opportunity to address the public anywhere at any time about my life story, I will gladly assume the podium as I know most people are out there of morbid curiosity.

Any murdered can get his or her name in the Newspaper but if a decent man wishes to announce to the world that he's lived happily with his wife for more than 30 years, he has to pay for it .

In my research I discovered that a female knee is an anatomical joint and not a public entertainment because there are some goddam thin women that a man could cut himself to death on their bones but you could not advise a man lost in the desert how to take a drink of water. To know a man, you have got to see him under stress where he's got to work for what he gets and then fight to keep it. If men must fight, they should fight clearly and honourably. None of us chooses to be born and the manner of our birth is beyond our control.

What we are searching for is ourselves – the hidden selves, buried inside us; buried invincible; inaccessible for the moment, waiting to be discovered. What can you do in this confusing world of contradictory signals? Contradictory and often dangerous if you misunderstand them from your Employers; your

Friends; those who Govern and even from your Relatives.

What can you do to make sense of the world? To make sense of the world, it sounds so simple but it is so difficult when you are already burdened with finding enough time for home; family and job; for a night out with friends; for reading a Newspaper or watching a Television Newscast to give you clues about the world you live in.

You are so busy. There are so many demands on you … How can you make sense of the world?

You begin to think you can't; you think you must leave it to the Experts because you think they have more time than you to look around to learn; you think they know more than you and after a while you just let them run things; you think you are not as good as they are. God has made you every bit as smart, every bit as wise as any other person in the world.

Listen to me! I know you! I have met you and talked with you in your homes; I've held your children on my lap; I've eaten at your tables. You are strong and good. There is so much in you to love; there is so much wisdom and thoughtfulness in you that you could do any job; fill any position in the world but you do not know this because you are afraid to know it.

Why are you afraid? What keeps you from going inside yourself and discovering and unlocking that other hidden self that I know is there because I have seen it.

You are afraid of the unknown. You are afraid that what you will discover may change your life as result it seems more comfortable to stay with what you know. Or you are that the person hidden within you is not the wise person you long for but an ignorant person, perhaps even an evil one.

You do not trust yourself, the self you have not yet met. Trust yourself! Believe in yourself; in the wisdom and goodness within you that God puts in all His creatures. And if you cannot yet believe; if you cannot yet trust yourself, trust God! Believe in God! He knows what you are capable of; He knows what lies ahead for you – self-discovery; joy; wisdom; love …
I know there is nothing you cannot do or understand or share with another. Trust me; believe in me and help me to help you!

Whatever you want to be is already inside you and whatever you want to be is waiting within your heart to be released hence my mission is to make my family happy; to give them the home and my love as well as protection. I will not allow to be pestered by meddling comments and question because what had come between us once, would again.

TRUTH WILL COME OUT

Always when Ganja
Is running short in Police Stations
The Police are raiding
Rastaman's houses
They will search and search for Ganja

We know that Ebumnandini Government
Is taking their Ganja to make profit
While they Rastafarians are rotting
In Prisons
Facing prosecution because they are
Protecting their crown; holy herb; sacrament
I remember when Rastafarian's mother
Facing prosecution after being arrested
To be in possession of Ganja.
She was healthy, later she became terminally ill
Shortly afterwards she died.
On the other hand, her son
A Rastafarian was facing charges for possession of Ganja
Facing jail; hardship and oppression

He was surprised to hear that
His mother has died
As he was in the Prison cell.
He will never forget what the Babylon
Has done to him.
He said: He will not quit smoking Ganja
Babylonians can even arrest him
100 times for Ganja and sentence him 80 times
He will not worry cause, Judgement Day
Is also coming for you Babylon
Because physically you are rich
But spiritually poor.

LIFE

Why is life so difficult?
Why is life not easy?
Our life is a shame
Our life is a curse or sin
Rastafari, we are suffering
Black man is dying

We are victims of the situation
We are consumed by Prisons every day
We left behind those who love us
They miss us every day '
They are grieving as if we are dead
They are crying like children

Do not cry my love
We will meet again
Do not lose hope
I will dry your tears away

Jah had never forsaken His children
He is going to guide and protect us
Until we meet again

I am a man in a non - ironic mask
Ganja man, Afri Jah
Jah Rastafari

I will survive even if I walk in the
Valley of the shadow of dead.
I fear no evil cause
Jah is with me
And He will comfort me.

In His secret place
Jah blessed and anointed
Black man's race
But Babylon shall perish.

CHAPTER 21

HOW TO DEAL WITH BACKSTABBING

According to my research done I discovered that when dealing with backstabbing, one should let his or her work speak for itself and be above reproach. He or She should be real in what he or she says and does. Treat others with the same respect he or she expects from them. He or She should not align him or herself with any group.

Keep your private life in private. Develop a thick skin and gather evidence of backstabbing. Stop and think before you speak. If you are a Supervisor or Manager and are aware of unhealthy gossip in the Office, take clear and decisive action by holding meetings. Find out if your Bosses are included in the unofficial line of communication. Finally, leave the Company or Department.

Regard your good name as the richest jewel that you can possibly be possessed of. For credit is like fire when once you have kindled it, you may easily preserve it but if you once extinguish it, you will it an arduous task to rekindle again. Ask me, the way to gain in a good reputation is to endeavour to be what you desire to appear, so said Socrates.

FACING A DISCIPLINARY HEARING

It is said, where a formal hearing is to be held; your Employer must give you at least 24 hours 'warning in advance by handing you a written charge. These charges should include Employer's documented evidence to be used against you as an Employee, the name(s) of the people who will be giving evidence; none of this was done in my case. Why?

The labour relations act stipulates that a dismissal is unfair if it is not affected for a fair reason and in accordance with fair procedure.

An Employee have a right to be granted reasonable time to prepare a defence. What about my case?
Once you have prepared your evidence, make sure the Chairperson is not your direct Supervisor or someone who has prior knowledge of the facts.

CCMA: MOVE 8 April 2015

WHAT TO DO BEFORE AND AT THE HEARING?

Read the charges carefully and be sure you understand them. What happened, where and when?

It is said: Splitting charges is unfair; for instance, charged with Fraud and being found guilty of Negligence. That is what happened in my cases both labour and criminal charges, why?

Employees have the right to be treated similarly for similar offences. Study the Company's Code of Conduct.

Do not plead guilty to something you did not do that could imply admission of the misconduct. The onus is on the Employer to prove the charges on a balance of probabilities.

The Chairman is seen as biased if seen together with the so-called Victim and evidence. Wo He! I was unfortunate due to lack of knowledge.

HOW TO PRAY

Prayer is the way you keep in constant contact with God. Use your own words in Prayer and overtime, you will become more comfortable talking with Him. Start out praying for a few minutes each day. Then ask God to give you desire to spend more time talking to Him.

You do not need to be in a special place to Pray. You should get used to praying anywhere and learn to Pray out loud and silently.

A good way to start Praying is by thanking God for all the things He has done for you. It is normal to Pray for the needs of your family; the people you love and others who are close to you. Ask God to meet their needs.

Talk to God about your life, your needs, and your problems. Ask for forgiveness for the wrong things you have done.

Spend time praising God and singing to Him. Take time to be silent and listen for God's voice - He wants to talk to you too.

Hebrews 3: 15 "So through Jesus we should never stop offering our sacrifice to God. That sacrifice is our praise coming from lips that speak His Name."

When we praise God, even when our minds resist, we are offering our best gift to God - a sacrifice. MEN.

NOTHING WILL COME OF NOTHING

In my research I discovered that the Roman calendar began formally with March. It is said, Julius Caesar helped to improve that Calendar hence his name was preserved in July.

The first Month of the year that is January is taken from the Roman god named Janus who was or still the god of beginning to whom this Month was sacred. February originated from Februa which was the festival of purification which occurred in this Month. March was named after Mars who was the Roman god of war.

April came from Aprilia, the Month when the earth opens, meaning aperio and this is my birth Month. May is said to have come from the Roman goddess called Maia who was the goddess of growth. June is believed to be originated from the Latin name Junius.

July originated from the name Julius Caesar who was born in this Month. August is said to be named in honour of Augustus Caesar. September is from the Latin word Septem, for this was the seventh Month of the Roman year.
October on the other hand is from the Latin word – Octo, for this was the eighth Month of the Roman year. November was the ninth Month of the Roman year and the Month is from the word Novem. December originated from the Latin word – Decem which was the tenth Month of the Roman year.

Nota bene, Ora pro nobis passim and get Quid pro quo pro bono public in bona fide as persona grata meaning, note well, pray for us here and there and get something in return in good fate or genuine as one in favour. That would be Modis-operandi meaning the manner of procedure in toto – in the whole or entirely.

In my research I also discovered how weekdays originated according to a certain Nom de plume - meaning the pen name or an Author's assumed name.

Monday is said to be the day of the Moon. Tuesday originated from the word Tiw's day of which Tiw is said to have been the old Northern god of war or martial honour. Wednesday is taken from the name or word "Woden's day" and it is said, Woden was the chief of the Northern gods.

Thursday originated from Thor's day and it is said, Thor was the Northern god of thunder. Friday came from the name Frigga's day and it is stated that, Frigga was the wife of Odin in Northern mythology.

Furthermore it is clearly stated that, Saturday originated from Saturn's day and Sunday is said to be the day of the Sun because in the olden days, people worshipped the Sun as the most importance in the world therefore Sunday was and still is the day of worship.

Do we picture all these as the truth? The glass is always half - full! Positive thoughts reduce stress and can even help improve our health - think positive! *Uthuleleni uyazizwa izindaba*? *Bayashumayela abafundisi*. *Wenzeni uma uqala lo nyaka*?

I learnt that, taking small Breaks during your work can be revitalising. Do an exercise for your neck for a few minutes or just sit comfortable doing nothing for a while! If you constantly feel anxious, try to write your thoughts down, go for a walk or have a cup of chamomile tea - it can help you relax. I also discovered that, position is important, for instance, standing or sitting up straight allow your muscles work efficiently and can also help improve your mood.

According to recent researchers, non-smokers who drunk 3 to 5 cups of coffee every day had 15 % lower death rates than those who did not drink coffee at all. *Wo Hhe*! *Amahlathi aphelile akusekho ukucasha* but exercise can make you feel better because it triggers the release of hormones called endorphins that can improve your mood.

Have you ever heard that the world's largest diamond was found in South Africa in 1905? The 3,106 - carat stone was called "Cullinan Diamond. "
And that Vredefort Dome in South Africa is the biggest and oldest meteorite impact that has been found? This meteorite fell on Earth more than 2000 million years ago. That the first human heart transplant was performed in 1967 a year after my birth year, by the South African Surgeon Christiaan Barnard in Cape Town.

Vilakazi Street in Soweto could be considered as the "Nobel Street" because Nelson Mandela and Desmond

Tutu who were awarded with the Nobel Peace Prize, lived there. It is also said, nine Nobel Prize winners were born in South Africa, and more than any other country in Africa, Nelson Mandela and Frederik Willem de Klerk are among them. I also discovered that, Tea is good for us! According to researchers drinking tea can help in protection against heart diseases.

Chapter 22

WHAT IS THE BEST MOVE?

The superiority complex and inferiority complex agree on one point. They are always on the useless side. Superiority may be on the useless or useful side of life hence criminality is the result of superiority complex and not the expression of fundamental and original viciousness.

If man fails to accept and endure freedom. He will then degenerate so that he is tempted to submit to an Authoritarian ideology such as Fascism. I believe that, man is not completely evil since he possesses many positive attributes such as the human ability to love. If productively expressed, it issues in the enhancement of his own interests and those of Society.

It is love which enables man to be sane because one of the consequences of the medieval Society was the creation in man a feeling of isolation from which modern man seeks to escape. If his escape is not accomplished through psychologically desirable channels such as humanistic communitarian socialism, then it will lead not to freedom but to Fascist ideology which is an escape effected by blind devotion to a leader or robotlike submission to all powerful State whose aggressive and sadistic program is levelled against minority groups.

It is said, man's life is determined by the inescapable alternative between regression and progression; between return to animal existence and arrival at human existence as a result, any attempt to return is painful and inevitably leads to suffering and mental sickness or to death either psychologically or mentally, which leads to insanity.

Every step forward is frightening and painful too, until a certain point has been reached where fear and doubt have only minor proportions. Aside from the physiologically nourished cravings like hunger, thirst, and sex, therefore all essential human cravings are determined by this polarity.

I realised that; man must solve a problem because he can never rest in the given situation of a passive adaptation to nature. The most powerful forces motivating man's behaviour stem from the condition of his existence which is the human situation. I learnt that, the sexual drive and all its derivations are no means the most powerful forces within man and their frustration is not the cause of mental disturbance.

Man cannot live statically because his inner contradictions drive him to seek for an equilibrium for a new harmony instead of the lost animal harmony with nature. After he has satisfied his animal needs, he is driven by his human needs of which his body tells him what to eat and what to avoid and his conscience ought to tell him which needs to cultivate and satisfy and which needs to let wither and starve out.

It came to my realisation that; hunger and appetite are functions of the body with which man is born conscience while potentially present requires the guidance of men and principles which develop only during the growth of culture. I also learnt that all passions and strivings of man are attempts to find an answer to his existence thus they are attempts to avoid insanity.

The real problem of mental life is not why some people become insane but rather why most avoid insanity. Another aspect of the human situation closely connected with the need for relatedness, is man's situation as a creature and his need to transcend this very state of the passive creature. Being endowed with reason and imagination, he cannot be content with the passive role of the creature which is the role of dice cast out of a cup.

He is driven by the urge to transcend the role of the creature which is the accidentalness and positivity of his existence by becoming a creator. I discovered that, a man can create life, and this is the miraculous quality which he indeed shares with all living things but with difference that he alone is aware of being created and of being a creator.

In the act of creation, man transcends himself as a creature, raises himself beyond the passivity and accidentalness of his existence into the realm of purposefulness and freedom. In man's need for transcendence lies one of the roots of love as well as for Art, Religion and Material production.

Love is one aspect of what I call the productive orientation as the active and creative relatedness of man to his fellow man: to himself and nature. This productive orientation is expressed in the proper grasp of the world by reason in the realm of thought. In the realm of action, the productive orientation is expressed in productive work like Art and Craftmanship. In the realm of feeling on the other hand, the productive orientation is expressed in love which is the experience of union with another person; with all men and with nature under the condition of retaining one's sense of integrity and independence.

Love paradoxically makes me more independent because it makes me stronger and happier; it makes me one with the loved person to the extent that individuality seems to be extinguished for the moment. In the experience of love lies the only answer to being human which is sanity. In loving, I experience "I am you "meaning, you the loved person; you the stranger and you everything alive.

If I love, I care meaning I am actively concerned with the other person's growth and happiness and I am not a Spectator. I am responsible because, I respond to his or her needs; to those he or she can express and more to those he or she cannot express because productive love always implies a syndrome of attitude; that of care; responsibility; respect and knowledge .

I discovered that, there is only one passion which satisfies man's need to unite himself with the world and to acquire at the same time a sense of integrity and individuality of which is love. For me, Love is union with somebody or something outside oneself under the condition of retaining the separateness and integrity of one's own self.

It is an experience of sharing, of communion which permits the full unfolding of one's own inner activity hence the experience of love does away with the necessity of illusions. Love is the experience of human solidarity with our fellow creatures. It is in the erotic love of man and woman; in the love of the mother and or for the child and in the love for oneself as a human being.

Love is the mystical experience of union because in the act of loving, I am one with all and yet I am myself; separate limited mortal being. Out of the very polarity between separateness and union, love is born and reborn.

I have discovered that, all men are idealists and cannot help being idealists, provided by idealism we mean, the striving for the satisfaction of needs which are specifically human and transcend the physiological needs of the organism. That sexual desire is notoriously fickle regarding its objects. Generally, sexual desire is precisely the force which helps the adolescent in his separation from mother and not the one which binds him to her.

The problem of Incest is not restricted to fixation to the mother because the tie to her is only the most elementary form of all-natural ties of blood which gave man a sense of rootedness and belonging. The ties of blood are extended to those who are blood relatives, whatever the system is according to which such relationships are established - the family and the clan; later on the State; Nation or Church assume the same function which the individual mother had originally for the child.

The individual leans on them; feels rooted in them; has his or her sense of identity as a part of them and not as an individual meaning a part from them thenceforth all cultures are religious and every neurosis is a private form of religion provided we mean by religion, an attempt to answer the problem of human existence.

All cultures provide for a patterned system in which certain solutions are predominant hence certain strivings and satisfactions. In my understanding, primitive religions - Theistic or Non - Theistic religions, they are all attempts to give an answer to man's existential problem. I also discovered in my research that, the finest as well as the most barbaric cultures have the same function, and the difference is only whether the answer given is better or worse.

I learnt that, man's birth as man means, the beginning of his or her emergence from his or her natural home, the beginning of the severance of his or her natural ties. This very severance is frightening because if he or she loses his or her natural roots that is "Where is he or she and who is he or she?" He or She would stand alone without a home; without roots and he or she could not bear the isolation and helplessness of this position and as a result, he or she would become insane.

Man can dispense with the natural roots only in so far as he or she finds new human roots and only after he or she has found them can he or she feel at home again in this world. Is it surprising to find a deep craving in man not to sever the natural ties; to fight against being torn away from nature; from mother; blood or soil?

I also discovered in my research that , the Psychoanalytic concepts to man as a social being in a social setting and that humanistic psychology is concerned with the individual as a member of Society to which he or she adjusts and contributes only in so far as he or she has sublimated his or her freedom instincts .

To create presupposes activity and care, it presupposes love for that which one creates. If a man cannot create life, he or she can destroy it. To destroy life makes him or her also transcend it. That man can destroy life is just as miraculous a feat as that he or she can create. For, Life is the miracle and the inexplicable.

Destructiveness is a secondary potentiality; rooted in the very existence of man and having the same intensity and power as any passion can have. I then realised that creation and destruction; love and hate are not two instincts which exist independently. They are both answers to the same need for transcendence and the will to destroy must rise when the will to create cannot be satisfied. However, the satisfaction of the need to create leads to happiness but destructiveness to suffering and most of all, for the destroyer him or herself.

The human existence is as much as the meaning of personal existence; a meaning which changes from man to man; from day to day and from hour to hour. Man does not fulfil the meaning of his or her existence merely by his or her creative endeavours and experiential encounters or by working and loving.

Man can be defined as the animal that can say "I"; that can be aware of him or herself as a separate entity but the animal being within nature and not transcending it but the animal has no awareness of itself; has no

sense of identity. Man has lost the original unity with nature; has to make decisions; is aware of him or herself and of his or her neighbour as different persons and he or she must be able to sense him or herself as the subject of his or her actions.
This need for a sense of identity is so vital and imperative that man could not remain sane if he or she did not find some way of satisfying it. Man's sense of identity develops in the process of emerging from the primary bonds which tie him or her to mother and nature.

The infant who is still with mother cannot yet say "I" nor has he or she any need for it. Only after he or she has conceived of the outer world as being separate and different from him or herself, does he or she come to the awareness of him or herself as a distinct being and one of the last words he or she learns to use is "I" in reference to him or herself.

Since I cannot remain sane without the sense of "I". I am driven to do almost anything to acquire this sense because behind the intense passion for status and conformity is this very need, and it is sometimes even stronger than the need for physical survival. In as much as I am not different, in as much as I am like the others and recognised by them as a regular fellow, I can therefore sense myself as "I".

Ahmed Kathrada once said: "The hardest thing to open is a closed mind." You live and learn, and you die and forget it all. Death may be the greatest of all human blessings hence Socrates once said: "The greatest way to live with honour in this world is to be what we pretend to be." Thus, in my understanding, Humanity takes itself far too seriously as it is and seriousness on the other and is the world's original sin. I discovered that, to comprehend cruelty is almost as difficult to understand love.

Have you ever heard of an old man who was cheating his wife for many years? It is said when he was very ill and about to die. He asked his wife to bring him his walking stick and his wife did as requested. On that stick he marked it with several green colours from the bottom to the top but fortunately he did not mark it up to the top but ended in the middle of a stick. He then confessed to his wife as he was afraid that he was about to die without making any confession to his wife for cheating. He then told her that from where he has marked on his walking stick, it indicates the number of times he has cheated with other women. But unfortunately, he did not die after his confession to his wife about his cheating with other women and recovered and became healthy again.

After a year, that old man's wife became very ill too and felt that she could die at any moment. She then remembered how her husband confessed his cheating to her and recovered. When she was very ill, she then called her husband and asked him to bring her, her

Holy Bible which was in her drawer. Her husband looked for the Bible but could not find it. He told her but she insisted that the Bible was there. After a long time, her husband told her that the only thing he finds in her drawer was only the outer cover of the Bible with no pages left. Her wife told him that, it was it that she was looking for and he should bring it to her.

After he has given it to her. She then said to her husband , she too has been cheating her husband and every time she cheated , she tore off one sheet from the Holy Bible hence the Bible has no sheets left in it because that was the number of times she has cheated her husband with other men therefore she asks for forgiveness . What do you think her husband will do? Forgive her or not?

Man is ready and willing to shoulder any suffering as soon and as long as he or she can see a meaning in it. What threatens man is his or her guilt in the past and his death in the future which are both inescapable, both he and she must accept. The man is confronted with the human condition in terms of fallibility and mortality. If man were immortal, he or she would be justified in delaying everything and there would be no need to do anything right now.

Man is called upon to make the best use of any moment and the right choice at any time. Be it that he or she knows what to do or whom to love or how to suffer as a result, having completed a task means having become eternal.

Man is torn away from the primary union with nature which characterizes animal existence, having at the same time, reason and imagination as he or she is aware of his or her aloneness and separateness; of his or her powerlessness and ignorance and of the accidentalness of his or her birth and of his or her death hence he or she could not face this state of being for a second.

If he or she could not find new ties with his or her fellow man which replace the old ones and regulated by instincts. Even if all his or her physiological needs were satisfied, he or she would experience his or her state of aloneness and individualism as a prison from which he or she had to break out in order to retain his or her sanity because the insane person is the one who has completely failed to establish any kind of union and is imprisoned even if he or she is not behind barred windows.

The necessity to unite with other human beings; to be related to them is an imperative need on the fulfilment of which man's sanity depends. This need is behind all phenomena which constitute the whole gamut of intimate human relations and of all passions which are called love.

I discovered several ways in which this union can be sought and achieved for instance; man can attempt to become one with the world by submission to a person;

to a group; to an Institution; to God … In this way he or she transcends the separateness of his or her individual existence by becoming part of somebody or something bigger than him or herself and experiences his or her identity in connection with the power to which he or she has submitted or man can try to unite him or herself with the world by having power over it, by making other a part of him or herself and thus transcending his or her individual existence by domination.

The Pessimist resembles a man who observes with fear and sadness how his or her wall Calendar from which he or she daily tears a sheet which resulted it to grow thinner and thinner with the passing days. A person who takes life in this sense is like a man who removes each leaf, files it carefully after having jotted down a few diary notes on it so that he or she can reflect with pride and joy on all the richness set down in these notes on all life he or she has already lived to the full.

Man finds him or herself surrounded by many puzzling phenomena and having reason. He or She has to make sense of them; has to put them in some context which he or she can understand and which permits him or her to deal with them in his or her thoughts hence the further his or her reason develops, the more adequate becomes his or her system of orientation and the more it approximates reality.

Even if man's frame of orientation is utterly illusory, it satisfies his or her need for some picture which is meaningful to him or her, whether he or she believes in the power of a totem animal; in a rain god or in the superiority and destiny of his or her race. Ultimately his or her need for some frame of orientation is satisfied.

What would be more obvious than the fact that people are willing to risk their lives; to give up their love; to surrender their freedom; to sacrifice their own thoughts; for the sake of being one of the herd; of conforming and of acquiring a sense of identity even though it is an illusory one.

The need for frame of orientation exists on two levels of which are: First and the more fundamental needs to have some frame of orientation regardless of whether it is true or false. Second level is the need to be in touch with reality by reason and to grasp the world objectively.

Reason is man's instrument for arriving at the truth. On the other hand, Intelligence is man's instrument for manipulating the world more successfully. As for me, Reason is essentially human, but Intelligence belongs to the animal part of man. The more man develops his or her objectivity, the more he or she is in touch with reality. The more he or she matures and the better he or she can create a human world in which he or she is at home.

In my understanding, Unreasonable or Immoral an action may be , man has an insuperable urge to rationalize it and to prove to him or herself and to others that his or her action is determined by reason or common sense or at least conventional morality . He or She has little difficulty to acting irrationally but it is almost impossible for him or her not to give his or her action the appearance of reasonable motivation.

In my research I also discovered that, every adult is in need of help; of warmth; of protection in many ways differing and yet in many ways similar to the needs of the child. The average adult has a deep longing for the security and rootedness which the relationship to his or her mother once gave him or her hence he or she cannot give up this intense longing unless he or she finds other ways of being rooted. All these has resulted for the possibilities a young person has or for his or her future. The older person on the other hand, has realities in the past; work done; love loved, and suffering suffered of which is something to be proudest of.

What man had done cannot be undone hence once an actuality, it is one forever. Everything in the past is saved from being transitory. If Architects want to strengthen a decrepit arch, they increase the load that is laid upon it, for thereby the parts are joined more firmly together.

The Universe is real, it is happening all the time; it is integral, and it is open to piece meal interpretation hence different men construe it in different ways. Since the Universe owes no prior allegiance to any man's construction system, it is always open to reconstruction.

I believe, not much is known about man. What is known relates mostly to Homo Sapiens as species and not to persons as known to others and to themselves. Man is a creature that responds to other man in as full sense as he or she responds to Oxygen or Gravity thus he or she is Anthroposcopy as Geotropic. Man is a nodal region; an organised field with a larger field; a region of perpetual interaction; a reciprocity of outgoing and incoming energies.

Man is the kind of creature that can love his or her mother Earth, the Sun and Stars beyond. He or She wondered of the beauty of the world and striven with tubes and numbers to fathom it all.

Personality on the other hand is actualised not only through his or her being drawn to other men but through his or her being drawn as an Artist; Scientist; Philosopher …

CHAPTER 23

WHEN THERE IS NO NEED TO DEFEND, THERE IS NO NEED TO ATTACK!

In my research I discovered Three ways in which man refuses to cooperate to be studied as the whole of which, One is that , his or her traits do not seem intelligible in their own right but they express something complicated going on inside . Two, some of the phases of this inner structure are hidden; pocketed off and oriented with respect to some long past situation which man had to control. Three, the man is reacting to something in the present that no one understands.

I also discovered that, Man's original temporality always refer to his or her disclosing and taking care of something. He or She carries out his or her existence in such caring for what is disclosed to him or her and he or she lasts from his or her past through his or her present into his or her future in letting things come forth and shine into the luminating realm of his or her existence and in caring for them in one way or the other. Existing in such a way, he or she is consuming his or her time.

Man is equipped to be this realm, for his or her task is to be both Servant and Shepherd of Beingness. If man lives, he or she is essentially and inevitably in debt. He or She is always and necessarily in arrears as far as carrying out his or her world in as far as disclosing possibilities of living are concerned. He or She is in arrears in two ways of which, one is being a finite man who can exist only in one of the world relations in which he or she is constituted at any given time. The other being, man's whole future waits for him or her until the moment of his or her death.

In my understanding, all actual concrete feelings of guilt and pangs of conscience are grounded in this existential being in debt. Instead of reflecting on something, we should let something speak for itself and we should express the thing as it is.

I realised that, a person looks at his or her world through self-made transparent patterns which he or she tries to fit over the world's realities hence the first and the most important aspects of self-experience of the ordinary child is that, he or she is loved by his or her parents and he or she perceives him or herself as lovable; worthy of love. His or Her relationship to his or her parents is one of affection hence the child experiences and values his or her experiences positively or negatively.

As experiences occur in life of the individual, they are either symbolized; perceived and organised into some relationship to the self or ignored because there is perceived relationship to the self – structure or denied symbolization because the experience is inconsistent with the structure of the self for instance, A woman whose concept of self has been deeply influenced by a very strict moralistic and religious upbringing, she experiences strong organic cravings for sexual satisfaction.

I learnt that, those elements which we control are regarded as a part of self but when such object as a part of our body is out of control, it is then experienced as being less part of the self, for instance : When a foot "goes to sleep" from lack of circulation, it becomes an object to us rather than a part of self of which proves that, the organic experience is something which occurs. It is an organic fact and symbolization of sexual desires hence they become part of conscious awareness that is something which conscious self can and does prevent.

In my understanding, there are seven stages of human growth of which, One and the first is Infancy which takes place a few minutes after birth. Followed by childhood by developing an ability to utter articulate sounds. Three, the stage of being a Juvenile when starting grammar School years. Followed by pre - Adolescence when he or she needs for an intimate relationship. Five, being an Adolescent, which varies from culture to culture, then followed by late - Adolescence when establishing a proper relationship and lastly which is a seventh stage of which is Adulthood or Maturity which leads to old age.

As the Infant develops, a portion of the total private world becomes recognised as "Me or I or Myself "thenceforth, there is no possibility of a sharp limit between experience of the self and the outside world. It is on this basis that Social Values are introjected from the culture for instance, an individual accepts from the culture, the value for example, One should neither have nor express feelings of jealous aggressiveness toward siblings. The value is then accepted because it is presumed to make for the enhancement of the individual to be a better and more satisfied person.

In my research, the human Infant is seen as having an inherent motivational system which he or she shares with all living things. A regulatory system - the valuing process which by its feedback keeps the organism on the beam of satisfying his or her motivational needs hence all organisms live in continuous communal existence and their necessary environment.

I discovered that, the living cannot live when separated from what may be described as their necessary environment and that, they maintain constant exchange through their bordering membranes with certain elements in the Physicochemical Universe around them and the interruption of this exchange in tantamount to death of the organism.

I then realised that any experience which is inconsistent with the Organisation or Structures of self may be perceived as a Threat. The more of these perceptions, the more rigidly the self-structure is organised to maintain itself for instance, a man may be criticized for a persistent failing. At the time he or she refuses to admit this experience at face value because it is too threatening to his or her self - Organisation and denies the fault as well as rationalizes the criticism but later alone, he or she rethinks the matter; accepts the criticism as just and revises his or her concept of self and consequently his or her behaviour.

The person who denies some experiences must continually defend him or herself against the symbolization of these experiences but when all experiences are available to consciousness and are integrated, then defensiveness is minimized. When there is no need to defend, there is no need to attack and when there is no need to attack then the other person is perceived for what he or she really is being a separate individual operating in terms of his or her own meanings based on his or her own perceptual field.

I learnt that, Values are always accepted because they are perceived as principles making for the maintenance, actualization and enhancement of the organism. As the organism strives to meet its needs in the world as it is experienced, the form which the striving takes must be a form consistent with the concept of self for instance, the person who regards him or herself as having no aggressive feelings cannot satisfy a need for aggression in any direct fashion.

In my opinion, the reaction is not to reality but to perception of reality for instance, a man in the desert will struggle just as hard to reach the "Lake" which he or she perceives in a mirage so as to reach a real waterhole. It is just like a horse sensing danger will try to reach the safety and security which he or she perceives in his or her stall even if the barn may be in flames. I believe therefore that, it the perception, not reality which is crucial in determining behaviour for instance, a man may strive for money as the source of emotional security even if it may not satisfy his or her needs.

I discovered that, the behaviour is not caused by something which occurred in the past but present tensions and present needs are the only ones which the organism endeavours to satisfy or reduce. It is true that, experience serves to modify the meaning which will be perceived in present experiences, yet there is no behaviour except to meet a present need.

When many of the organic experienced needs are refused admittance to consciousness due to the inconsistent with the concept of self, then the pressure of the organic need may become so great that the organism initiates its own seeking behaviour and brings about satisfaction of the need without ever relating the seeking behaviour to the concept of self.

The organised character of the behaviour grows out of the fact that the organism on a Physiological basis can initiate and carry on complex behaviour to meet its needs for instance , A boy whose upbringing created a self - concept of purity and freedom from base sexual impulses was arrested for lifting the skirts of two little girls and examining them . He insisted that, he could not have performed this behaviour. When presented with witness, he was positive by saying that: "I was not myself."

Well! His memory says that He did it, His pride says He couldn't have done it but, in the end,, His memory yields.

In my understanding, Defensiveness is a process by which accurate symbolization of threatening experiences are prevented from reaching awareness.

Autism on the other hand, is the movement of cognitive processes in the direction of need satisfaction.

This to me indicates that, the developing sexuality of an Adolescent boy and the accompanying curiosity constituted a strong organic need for which there seemed no channel of satisfaction which was consistent with the concept of self. Eventually the organism behaved in such a way as to gain satisfaction but this behaviour was not felt to be nor was it a part of the self and over which the boy exercised no conscious control, which shows that, emotion accompanies and in general it facilitates goal - directed behaviour.

Behaviour is basically the goal - directed attempt of the organism to satisfy its needs as experienced in the private world as perceived. It may in some instances be brought about by organic experiences and needs which have not been symbolized. Such behaviour may

be inconsistent with the structure of the self but in such instances, statements like: "I didn't know what I was doing, or I really wasn't responsible for what I was doing."
It also happens regarding snoring or restless behaviour during sleep. For that reason, the self is not in control and the behaviourist not regarded as part of self.

The intensity of the emotional reactions appears to vary according to the perceived relationship of the behaviour to the maintenance and enhancement of the organism , thus if my leap to the curb to escape the oncoming automobile is perceived as making the difference between life and death , it will be accompanied by strong emotion .

In my understanding, behaviour is a reaction to the private world as perceived. The best vantage points for understanding behaviour is from the internal frame of reference of the individual him or herself.

Communication on the other side of the coin, is always faulty and imperfect because only in a clouded fashion can we see the world of experience as it appears to the individual.

There is no such thing as a difference without a likeness being implied and vice versa, for instance, Threat is experienced when upheaval confronts the core structure of an individual's world view. Aggression on the other side is viewed as the pursuit of constructive experience, but Hostility is a desperate attempt to validate discredited personal constructs and Guilt erupts because of being dislodged from one's role.

I discovered that, Freedom from inner tension or psychological adjustment exists when the concept of Self is at least roughly congruent with all the experiences of the organism for instance, The woman who perceives and accepts her own sexual cravings and also perceives and accepts as part of her reality the cultural values placed upon suppression of these cravings, will be accepting and assimilating all the sensory evidence experienced by the organism in this connection. This is possible only if her concept of self in this area is broad enough to include both her sex desires and her desire to live in some harmony with her culture.

In my experience, I discovered that the behaviour can be shaped into new pattern to some extent by rewarding and punishing consequences and that learning would be exceedingly laborious and hazardous if it proceeded solely on this basis.

People can be effectively conditioned through the experience of others and that Observers who repeatedly witness the sequence of events begin to show emotional responses to the tone alone even through no pain is ever inflicted on them.
The nature of the relationship between the Observer and the Sufferer is undoubtedly an influential factor.

People are generally less affected emotionally by the adversities of strangers than by the suffering and joy of those close to them and on whom they depend hence people can easily frighten themselves by fear provoking thoughts and they can become sexually aroused by generating erotic fantasies.

I discovered that, many phobic behaviours arise not from actual injurious experiences with the phobic objects but rather from witnessing others either by responding fearfully toward or be hurt by certain things.

Observed consequences provide reference standards that determine whether a particular reinforce that is externally administered will serve as a reward or as punishment. Incentive contrast effects resulting from discrepancies between observed but directly experienced consequences received relatively little attention.

People repeatedly observe the actions of others and the occasions on which they are rewarded ; ignored or punished then the vicarious reinforcement is a change in the behaviour of Observers resulting from seeing the response consequences of others but vicarious punishment is indicated when observed negative consequences and reduce people's tendency to behave in similar or related ways .

Witnessing aggression punished usually produces less imitative aggression than seeing it obtain social and material success or go unnoticed. Observed and directly experienced punishment may be equally effective in reducing deviant behaviour but seeing transgression go unpunished seems to heighten analogous actions in Observer to the same degree as witnessing models rewarded.

In my research I discovered that, Conscious acceptance of impulses and perceptions greatly increases the possibility of conscious control. It is therefore for this reason that the person who has come to accept his or her own experiences also acquires the feeling of being in control of him or herself for instance, when a person finds his or her personal construction failing him or her, he or she suffers anxiety but when he or she faces an impending upheaval in his or her core structure , he or she experiences threat and when he or she finds him or herself dislodged from his or her role, he or she experiences guilt .

Chapter 24

MAN IS TODAY'S GREAT PROBLEM

In my research I discovered that , there are three types of physical constitution of man , each with its correspondent temperament of which One is Mesomorphic Constitution with its Somatotopic temperament which are aggressive; assertive; energetic; dominating; ruthless; loud; manic; active and fond of risks. Two is the Ectomorphic with its Cerebrotonic temperament which are tense; restrained; sensitive; secretive and inhibited. A person under this type recoils from social situations, particularly those in which he or she must make new acquaintances and he or she is introverted. Three is Endomorphic Constitution with its Viscerotropic temperament in which a person is relaxed;

gluttonous; readily sociable; dependent and complacent.

Personology meaning Psychology of Personality has brought to my attention that, the person has inner forces which are needs or instincts; urges and drives. I would only focus to two types of needs of which are Primary or Viscerogenic needs which are engendered and instilled by characteristic periodic bodily events. They do with physical satisfaction like air; water; food; sex; urination; defecation; lactation.

The other is Secondary or Psychogenic needs which has not subjectively localizable bodily origins. They are occasioned by regnant tensions with or without emotion. They are closely dependent upon certain external conditions or upon images depicting these conditions and they do with mental or emotional satisfaction.

I learnt that; one need succeeds another because a need is a latent attribute of an organism. If the proper conditions are provided, the need will be activated. The Physiologically conditioned needs are not the only imperative part of man's nature but there is another part just as compelling which is the need to be related to the world outside oneself and which is also a need to avoid aloneness because to feel completely alone and isolated leads to mental disintegration just as physical starvation leads to death.

How can I be a good man? How can I live a good life? How can I be fruitful or happy or at peace with myself?

With these age - old questions, I learnt that, Individuals can be healthier, even much healthier than the culture in which they grow and live as they have an ability to be detached from their surroundings therefore he or she lives by his or her inner laws rather than by outer pressures.

Healthy individuals are not externally visible. They are not marked off by unusual clothes or manners or behaviour. It is an inner Freedom that they have and for that reason, external Freedom is less important than inner Freedom because healthy organism already having enough salt, do not specially crave or need it.

An organism needs salt to attain health and avoid illness, so does it need love for the same reason. The organism is designed that it needs salt and love in the same way that Automobiles are designed that they need gas and oil.

The organism has a vaguely delineated, intrinsic nature of its own. It is then quite clear that this inner nature is a very delicate and subtle something rather than being strong and overpowering as it is in lower animals which are never in any doubt about what they are; what they want and what they don't want.

The organism does not develop to the full of its capacity for suffering pain nor does the human individual develop or actualize his or her capacity for terror or his or her capacity for vomiting. I then realised that the organism actualizes itself in the direction of greater differentiation of organs and of function. It moves in the direction of limited expansion through growth; expansion through extending itself by means of its tools and expansion through reproduction.

The organism again moves in the direction of greater independence or self - responsibility hence its movement is in the direction of an increasing self - government; self - regulations and away from control by external forces. It moves through struggle and pain toward enhancement and growth as it does not operate smoothly in that direction.

The whole process may be symbolized and illustrated by the child's learning to walk. The first steps often involve struggle and usually painful, but the immediate reward involved in taking few steps is no way commensurate with pain of falls and bumps and a child may also revert to crawling for a time because of the pain.

The forward direction of growth is more powerful than the satisfactions of remaining infantile as the child will actualize him or herself despite the painful experiences in so doing. In the same way, he or she will become independent; responsible; self - governing and socialised despite the pains which are involved in these steps. Even when he or she does not because of a variety of circumstances and the exhibit growth of these are more complex sorts but one may still rely on the fact that , the tendency is present and this tendency will still operate if given the opportunity for Clear - cut choice between forward - moving and regressive behaviour.

It is said , Free choice from among wide range of possibilities has been found useful in such diverse social situations like , choosing roommates in an Institution or choosing Teachers or Courses because tolerance and freedom of taste as well as opinion are the key necessities hence normality as an ideal is not an unattainable goal set out far ahead of us - it is actually within us meaning it is existent but hidden as potentiality rather than invented and based on empirical findings than on hopes or wishes.

In my understanding, a good environment must change to stress spiritual and psychological rather than material and economic forces. If the individual has enough intelligence to create problems for him or herself, he or she ought to have enough to extricate him or herself with the aid of a Counsellor because there are no intellectual problems but emotive and value problems lie at the root of a person's maladjustment.

Everyone is faced with his or her own peculiar problems, consequently in treatment because no single concept will prove to be the source of all maladjustment except “Oedipus complex.”

I therefore suggest that, an emphasis must be placed on the individual’s immediate situation rather than the past because in my understanding, the lack of an individualized system of values which is acceptable to the individual as well as harmonious with the values of his or her Society is basic in all maladjustment for instance, a thirsty man walking along the desert sands will run as eagerly to a pool of water which is only a mirage as he or she will to a real pool.

Every individual exists in a continually changing world of experience of which he or she is the Centre because reality is basically the private world of individual perceptions. Though, for social purpose, reality consists of those perceptions which have a high degree of commonality among various individuals for instance, most people in our culture would have a perception of it which is very similar to my own.

I discovered that, when perception changes, the reaction of the individual changes too, for instance, as long as a parent is perceived as a domineering individual , that is the reality to which the individual reacts but when he or she is perceived as a rather pathetic individual trying to maintain his or her status , then the reaction to this new reality is quite different.

The organism on the other hand reacts to the private world or phenomenal field as it is experienced and perceived. I do not react to absolute reality but to my perception of this reality because it is this perception which for me is reality. Let me cite an example of two individuals who listen to Radio speech made by a political candidate about whom they have no previous knowledge, and they are both subjected to the same auditory stimulation.

One will perceive the candidate as a demagogue, a trickster or a false prophet and will be reacting accordingly. The other One will receive him or her as a leader of the people, a person of high aims and purpose. In other words, each is reacting to the reality as he or she perceived it.

Another example, two young parents perceive differently the behaviour of their offspring just like the Son and Daughter have different perception of their parents. These shows that, the behaviour in the above instances is appropriate to the reality as perceived.

For me, Reality is for the individual. His or Her perception for instance, The Psychotic who perceives that his or her food is poisoned or that some malevolent group is out to "get" him or her, react to his or her reality as perceived in much the same way You and I would respond if we perceived t our food as contaminated or our enemies are plotting against us.

The organism reacts as an organised whole to this private world which is also known as phenomenal field hence the organism is at all times a total organised system in which alteration of any part may produce changes in any other part . For instance, a man who feels that his security in his or her work is being seriously threatened, develops hatred.

I learnt that, the most basic characteristic of organic life is its tendency toward total; organised and goal - directed responses which is evidenced by the fact that, when one Avenue is blocked off, the animal organises to utilise another Avenue to the same goal.

I discovered that, we live by a perceptual Map, that is, words or symbols which are never reality themselves. This is the concept to keep in mind, for it may help to convey the nature of the world in which the individual lives. The following is the practical example of what I am talking about:

The food that lies behind doors of the end of a Maze so that neither smell nor sight can reach it, is not part of the life space of the animal. The individual will only start his or her journey if he or she thinks the food is there even if it is not there. A person will not move toward the food which is at the end of the Maze if he or she does not know it is there. This proves that the degree of expectation also influences man's behaviour as a result knowledge affects behaviour. Another example can be that, if one wishes to safeguard a child's education during the year, one will have to calculate his or her future.

My question is: Which one should or has to be considered under the following reaction?

If an individual sit in a room, trusting that the ceiling will come down. Should only his or her subjective probability be considered for predicting behaviour or should we consider the objective probability of the ceiling's coming down as determined by Engineers. I think, only the first must be considered.

The individual is the only one who can know how the experience was perceived for instance, I can never know with vividness or completeness how a failure on an examination is experienced by you hence the world of experience is for each individual a private world.

It is true that, a large portion of this world of experience is available to consciousness and may become conscious if the need of the individual causes certain sensations to come into focus because they are associated with the satisfaction of a need.

CHAPTER 25

HAS MAN BECOME SEPARATE FROM NATURE?

The boundary conditions of the life space during long as well as short time periods depend partly on the actions of the individual him or herself hence food habits do not occur in empty space but they are part and parcel of the daily rhythm of being awake and asleep; of being alone in a group; of earning a living and playing; of living in a hot or cold climate and so on. This proves that some forces support each other; some oppose each other; some are driving forces and others are restraining forces.

A live process like river which moves but keeps a recognizable form, meaning, we must deal in group life as in individual life of which in Physics is known as "quasi - stationary process ". It means that, a person's structure is often relatively constant over a long period of time, nevertheless a great change in the environment as falling in love; being converted or some other decisive events can bring about a far reaching change of structure which may be either temporary or lasting.

This relatedness to others is not identical with physical contact because an individual may be alone in a physical sense for many years and yet he or she may be related to ideas; values or at least to social patterns that give him or her a feeling of communion and belonging . Moral aloneness is the lack of relatedness to Values; Symbols and Patterns therefore moral aloneness is as intolerable as the physical aloneness as a result, the kind of relatedness to the world may be noble or trivial.

Men cannot live without some sort of co -operation with others if he or she wants to survive whether for the purpose of defending him or herself against enemies or dangers of Nature in order that, he or she may be able to work and produce.

Each person experiences this need for the help of others very drastically as a child on the account of the factual inability of the human child to take care of him or herself with regard to all important functions such as communication with others is a matter of life and death for the child and the possibility of being left alone is necessary the most serious threat to the child's whole existence.

Unless the child or man belonged somewhere; unless his or her life has some meaning and direction , he or she would feel like a particle of dust and be overcome by his or her individual insignificance as a result he would not be able to relate him or herself to any system which would give meaning and direction to his or her and he or she would be filled with doubt and this doubt would eventually paralyze his or her ability to act but also to live.

I discovered that, there are certain factors in man's nature which are fixed and unchangeable which are the necessity to satisfy the physiologically conditioned drives and the necessity to avoid isolation and moral aloneness. In the process of dynamic adaptation to culture, several powerful drives develop which motivate the actions and feelings of the individual.

The individual may or may not be conscious of these drives but in any case, they are forceful and demand satisfaction once they have developed. They become powerful forces which in their turn become effective in moulding the social process.

Man has become separate from Nature because he or she has taken the first step toward becoming human by becoming an individual. The more the man gains Freedom in the sense of emerging from original oneness with man and nature, the more he or she becomes an individual and he or she has no choice but to unite him or herself with the world in the spontaneity of love and productive work or else seek a kind of security by such ties with the world and destroy his or her Freedom as well as the integrity of his or her individual self.

The emergence of man from Nature is a long - drawn process to the large extent he or she remains tied to the world from which he or she emerged; he or she remains part of Nature - the Soil he or she lives on; the Sun; the Moon and Stars; the Trees and Flowers; the Animals and the group of people with whom he or she is connected by the ties of blood. Animate and Inanimate Nature are part of his or her human world as he or she is still part of the natural world.

Human existence and Freedom are from the beginning inseparable. Man is born without the Equipment for appropriate action which the animal possesses and he or she is dependent on his or her parents for a longer time than any animal. His or Her reactions to his or her surroundings are less quick and less effective than the automatically regulated instinctive actions are.

He or She goes through all dangers and fears which this lack of instinctive equipment implies. This very helplessness of man is the basis from which human development springs thenceforth man's biological weakness is the condition of human culture.

Biblically, Man's expulsion from Paradise emphasises the suffering resulting from this act of transcending Nature, to be alienated from Nature and from another human being hence we find man naked and ashamed. He or she is alone and free, yet powerless and afraid thus the newly won Freedom appears as a curse because he or she is free from the sweet bondage of Paradise but he or she is not free to govern him or herself and to realise his or her individuality.

In my research I also discovered that, Three Modes of world are three simultaneous aspects of the world which characterize the existence of each one of us as being in the world. One is UMWELT meaning world around, which is a biological world, generally called Environment. Two is MITWELT meaning with - world, which is the world of beings of one's own kind - the world of one's fellow men and the Third one is EIGENWELT meaning own - world , which is made of relationship to one's self. I then realised that we as human beings are living in all three of them simultaneously.

In my research I learnt that, to the degree to which the individual has not yet completely severed the Umbilical cord which fastens him or her to the outside world, he or she lacks Freedom but these ties give him or her security and a feeling of belonging and of being rooted somewhere. These ties that exist before the process of individuation and resulted in the complete emergence of an individual are called Primary ties.

They are organic in the sense that, they are part of normal human development and they imply a lack of individuality, but they also give security and orientation to the individual. They are ties that connect the child with his or her mother; the member of the primitive Community with his or her Clan; Nature; the medieval man with the Church and his or her social Caste.

Once this stage of complete individuation is reached and the individual is free from these Primary ties, he or she is confronted with a new task to orientate and root him or herself in the world and to find security in other ways than those which were characteristic of his or her pre - individualistic existence.

Freedom then has a different meaning from the one it had before this stage of Evolution is reached. The more the child grows and to the extent to which Primary ties are cut off. The more he or she develops a quest for Freedom and Independence.

The dialectic quality in this process of growing individuation has two aspects which are that the child grows stronger physically and emotionally plus mentally.

In each of these spheres, intensity and activity grow. At the same time, these spheres become more and more integrated as a result, an organised structure guided by the individual's will and reason develops.

The other aspect of the process of individuation is growing aloneness. When one has become individual, one stands alone and faces the world in all its perilous overpowering aspects and impulses arise to give up one's individuality; to overcome the feeling of aloneness and powerlessness by completely submerging oneself in the world outside.

Phylogenetically which means that the history of man can be characterized as a process of growing individuation and growing freedom. Man emerges from the pre - human stage by the first steps in the direction of becoming free from coercive instincts. By instinct I refer to a specific action pattern which is determined by inherited neurological structures thus a clear-cut trend can be observed in the animal kingdom.

The lower an animal is in the scale of development; the more are its adaptation to nature and all its activities controlled by instinctive and reflex action mechanisms. The higher an animal is in the scale of development, the more flexibility of action pattern and the less completeness of structural adjustment do we find at birth. This development reaches its peak with such, but the man is the most hopeless of all animals at birth because his or her adaptation to nature is based essentially on the process of learning and not on instinctual determination.

The human needs for love; knowledge or for a philosophy are weak and feeble rather than unequivocal and unmistakable. They whisper rather than shout. I discovered that, man suffers hunger or suppression but he or she does not suffer from the worst of all pains which are complete aloneness and doubt because he or she is a light which luminates whatever particular Being comes into the realm of its rays.

You must love me; protect me; forgive me and not desert me because I am so weak and helpless. The deprivation of love leads to illness. These illnesses if they have not gone so far as to be irreversible, they are curable. The crying of infants tells us that, they prefer affection to non - affection.

Circumstances dictate that I must now tell you of the extra - ordinary message that, the Church is human and that is its flaw but that is also its strength and its beauty.

I realised also that, those hideous; wicked and scurrilous girls know the difference between kissing and fucking but they ignore the fact that, abortion is murder; that abortion is the unforgivable sin hence I believe in God the Father; Jesus and the blessed Mother.

Oh! God give me strength. They are very close to reaching their limits. They must have made a mistake when they chose me as their target. They had gotten under my skin the second I saw them. The people heard the story in bits and pieces hence they caught me off guard. They got it big time as something completely unexpected happened to me, all because of the insecure Employer turning adversity to his advantage. Like iron filings are attracted to a magnet, so were my thoughts drawn straight to my Principal. As a result, I found myself doing something I could not remember having done for many years that is Praying on daily basis.

I am working hard on this but not getting very far .To be honest , I'd never experienced anything like this before , because my conviction story had certainly caught fire in a hurry because they all tried to nail me down . Who was my mouthpiece pertaining all this nonsense? Someone was reluctant to take any kind of stand, but he or she knew that the story was going to come out one way or the other. When the Newspapers came out behind my back, they were still as warm as a loaf of fresh baked bread. Hell! These papers were hot!

I felt no fear for him or her, only for the void my conviction would create. My terror was for the people. I wondered in all humility how I had failed God. How I had been so early defeated? Shooting pains engulfed my heart like knives piercing into my chest but I believe, they are going to an early grave with their precious secret and they are going straight to the kingdom of hell but I put it out of my mind now. I tried to anyway. Years and Months had passed but of course I could not forget.

I did not want to relive the heart-breaking experience hence I was trying to keep the story quiet. Why did they become in the first place for dropping their little Bombshell?

Small mindedness clung to the people like tar to a wooden spoon. For few days, my mind went completely blank because I could not believe that I'd broken the rules and that a door seemed to slam shut on the newly formed trust between us.

I now know the unthinkable as it had taken me so much courage to be where I am currently in the first place. I believe I am not the first one to go through this kind of thing and certainly I will not be the last. I could act crazy if I wanted to, but I felt lost; a little confused and very tired because I could not make sense of it and that bothered the hell out of me.

Well! They were not just smart, but they were also cleverer because they are keeping tabs on me for a reason, apparently the reason would arrive.

What is happening in Ebumnandini? What could I possibly say that would make people believe me?

All I want is everything to be logical and clear and sane hence I am trying to make sense out of this.

I am dead serious, and I am dead right but there is nothing earth shattering to report so far. So, it goes.

It was like guns fighting against spears as they were ready to use any pressure and any weapon to gain their ends. I still remember it vividly and I curse the memory. I cannot or never forget a grudge until I have buried both grudge and enemy in the same grave. I do not know what they intend but I must go to find out. I have no choice in the matter as I can do nothing else.

CHAPTER 26

I AM WHAT I SAY

Who can tell about the ways of God? Who can truly understand? I certainly cannot but I reject evil with all my strength. I reject evil! I reject evil! Who will pray for us sinners now and the hour of death? I believe that, evil is powerful and tangible force on earth. Evilis real as you and I are real. Even today, the devil exists. The devil is a brilliant imitator, a master of perverse mimicry. He or She can seem not be anywhere but he or she is everywhere.

Those who deny the existence of evil, supposedly on a rational basis, are denying what they see in the world especially here in our so-called Democratic Ebumnandini; they are denying what they hear about; what they think and feel almost every day of their lives . They are denying what they read in Newspapers and watch on Televisions. Believe me, evil is all around us right now. I know this to be true. You must fear the devil, not the words I am saying.

This is the scariest time ever on earth and the Holy Bible has provided clues in the Apocalyptic writings that , the Child of the devil must be destroyed and the Child of God must be protected at any cost by us - any cost! We will only know what to do when the time comes.

The study of our Lady - Mary, the mother of Jesus Christ leads directly back to Eve and lays bare the whole subject of sex. The virgin - Mary who many and increasing millions feel should be elevated to the level of her Son - Jesus Christ. Eve on the other hand was tempted by the serpent and ate the fruit of the forbidden tree, was cast out of the Garden of Eden. In my understanding, Eve had accepted Satan and our lady - Mary would crush him or her.

According to two major theories called by Scholars of Christian tradition indicates that, Mary herself was conceived immaculately inside the womb of her mother. This indicates that, she had been born without original sin. The other theory indicates that, when Mary died perhaps in the ancient City of Ephesus in Western Asia Minor, her body and soul ascended into Heaven. This was called "The Assumption of the Blessed Virgin."

It is really amazing that, Mary - the Virgin and the Blessed mother of Jesus Christ was and still is the least known by far most mysterious of all Biblical figures. Why? In my understanding, Mary was a woman and a mother, but the Scripture Writers were men. Maybe some things had changed since the birth of Jesus Christ.

Christians all over the world believes in the Virgin birth and that Jesus Christ, the Son of God had become man. Is it the truth or is it a myth? All I want is the simple unvarnished truth. Isn't it what we all are searching for?

Did you know that the evil's presence is sometimes called monoloch or mormo which means king of Ghouls or Beelzebub meaning lord of flies? It is said in some parts of Africa, people call him "Damballa" meaning the beast.

I feel as if I have stepped into the pages of the Bible as I have a feeling that, the devil is to be born as human child very soon as currently there is an epic battle between good and evil. I believe that, I will defeat Satan because he can be beaten, and he is after all a fallen Angel.

The devil is everywhere, even in the Holy See. He or She seems invincible but is everywhere.

Christianity on the other hand is based on a belief in miracles. Have you ever heard about two Virgins who were thousands of moles apart? One girl would bear the Son of God, the Saviour and the other girl would bear the son of Satan?

My head is still ringing from my brief disturbing dismissal and at the same my conviction. I was mistrustful of Just about everything. I also needed to know what terrible thing had happened between me and the so-called "Complainant" on that specific day. When it came right down to it, nothing made complete sense as a result, everything required some faith in my part - Faith! It always came down to that. My questions were and still are: What am I here in Prison to find out and what mystery still had to unravel?

Dear Father in Heaven, I am your humblest servant. I know, you can feel my sadness and my love for You. Father, I am so lonely now. I am so terribly lonely these ongoing years. I have a beautiful and very special passion for life. I and the said "Complainant", my class ex – learner, were not a couple and we were far from it. It was as if there was a thick wall of live electric current between us which was both attracting and repelling simultaneously. I am intellectually open to all possibilities and realised that she knows no shame. She is the salt of the earth and the backbone necrophilia meaning of the Empire. I had to dust my feet off and leave because I believe, when I am abused, I know that I have touched the stars.

I could almost remember that I was bombed out of my mind, but it kept fading away. I guess, someone watched over me like a hawk from the beginning to end and that was my final stop before I go any further with my future. If there is any help in this world, it would come from her or them as the cataclysmic events are piling up one on top of the other because the past has no future thus for me failure is so much more interesting than success .

I knew at once that they could knock the wind out of me just about anytime they wanted to do with a few little words because when I met them on the streets, I could tell that they were trying to mask their guilty consciousness and hurt; their calm calculating expressions were jarring and I could see it in their lying coward's eyes because I could see right through them.

I am being impulsive and bull - headed had no patience with their devious methods as a result I gave off an indisputable "don't mess with me" attitude. I have no reason to lie therefore I can no longer spare the catalogue of their transgressions. They know very well what stories and scandals have been put about. The whole country - Mnandi especially Ekukhanyeni Province knows them. This is for me, an appointed time for the people to learn the truth as I am also eager to know my fate.

It is getting harder and harder not to believe in something. Either in good or in evil? I had not asked for this. I had not done anything to deserve it. This whole thing has gotten out of hand because just remembering made me hurt so bad, but I could not turn back the clock even though I had more at stake here than my own life.

Nothing in my life has prepared me for this. Nothing in my family's lives has prepared them for this either. All I wanted desperately was to feel safe and warm and normal, not to be afraid and not to be paranoid. Please God, bless me and my family and take care of us. *Ngizinikela kuwe izitha zami, Baba*! I love my family even more now than I had before being in these difficulties. I have been through the most terrifying times and that has gotten me and my family very close in a short period of time because No one in Authority would ever answer my questions about anything as I was always kept in the dark.

I need to know how to prepare myself. The search for the truth. I truly need your help, there is so very much at stake for so many people around the country. I cannot do this job alone, please, you must help me. I have no free choice left as I am currently having no freedom of thought, no freedom of action due to a black monolith with an unknown agenda.

I definitely want you to hear mystery as something bad happened in and around our School - Phakama Secondary; something insane for instance, on the day of my conviction, the Fog had grown thick , obscuring everything beyond the car's headlights as we sped from Esibayeni to Umhlola Regional Court. I cannot deny what I have seen with my own eyes and what I have done and moulded with my own hands. I knew that, children often experience life as magical but also as threatening even though I was always kept in the dark.

I could not help feeling concerned and afraid. Too many bad things had happened already. The pain was and still is unbearable as if my skull were being ripped apart as a result I fear that my descent into hell has already began because I forgot about menace outside and I thought only of my family and their safety.

I had two choices that is walk away or take my chances. I was and still is right even though I was so jumpy and could not keep my hands still and my mind was on the indescribable moment. My whole world narrowed, and my skin became as cold as ice. I was and still feeling time as both too fast and too slow, but the excruciating wait is almost over, but I am still unprepared for the unknown.

I sometimes lost track of time and wondered how I could have been so stupid. People don't understand the facts of the situation and I felt and still feel that I could see right into their souls. I repeatedly said, I am innocent. If no one believes me, what will happen to me and my family as well as to my future?

It is too late for recriminations or regrets. I had never been more afraid for my life or my soul. If you help me now, you will know everything soon. Every twist and infernal turn and trick of the abominable beast. Isn't it obvious as the nose on your faces?

Something unearthly is happening but Satan cannot hurt me, not here on earth but only in hell. I am too strong! I am a special person! I do not fondle and kissing young girls. I am not a pig. Do I look like an ugly animal, forcing myself on my learners or young girls? This is an insult to me. I would not do it. I did not do anything wrong to her. Don't you believe me?

Is this to be the future pattern of my life, this progress from easy successful and happy life to drabness and poverty? If you do not know and cannot guess, it is not my task to enlighten you. It was and still is some matter important enough to have cut the ground from under me; distorting my whole future and I must get to the bottom of it.

I was prosecuted and convicted with no facts; no concrete evidence but just feelings and I was swept up in them and imprisoned after being unfairly dismissed from work. Should I be looking at the other side of the coin? I am hungry for answers because I have had wounds already today and one more will not be the death of me.

I believe, I was in Prison for a purpose as a result I am the bravest of all and I felt at the mercy of whoever or whatever laid claim to me whilst in such difficulties. The stigma of "Criminality "undreamed-of; unimaginable had touched me fatally. It was and still is like some black bird of ill omen was sitting on my shoulders and announcing to all the world that I was and still is impure. While anger on one side and pride on the other ebbed and flowed between us, then I remembered this song: "*Wena uzamana nempilo yami.*"

I had some thoughts during this time of solitude, and none can change my mood because my anger overtopped all other emotions. I then realised that there must be troubles ahead of me; great changes to made and to be endured. At least there was my beloved wife and family. I would therefore not burden myself with the clutter of the past, but I would shake as much dust as I could off shoes. Remember, I have been thinking, not drinking because I believe, what is said when drunk, was thought when sober. As a result, I made them as silent as the dead because I am also having a breaking point if they want me to because I am what I say.

How can I live a normal life again? I am now breaking the silence because I believe, it is the only way of outfacing my opponents. "*Basheshe bahleka, ngeke kuhlale kunjena.*" Even though my small burst of joy was tainted by anxiety but I am still flailing my arms , trying to swat away an invincible presence because everything happened in great numbers , false allegations; dishonesty; lies of Newspapers about my so said “Case”; suspension from work; incomplete labour hearings; biasness of Prosecutors and Department of Education Officials; conflict of interest between SADTU members, Attorneys and Scorpion Legal Department; disappearance of Attorney and Appeals … as a result I felt like the hot knives were lancing into my heart because everything felt bizarre . I felt homesickness as grief because I was away from home.

For me, the Sea is the Universe, and it is eternal, and my so-called “Foes” are like dead fish in the sack. The sooner that is realised, the better for all concerned. I trust only myself; it is the only sane thing to do.

In my opinion, teachers are not to be turned out at a snap of the fingers like trespassing beggars or dogs ordered to the stables. I still had plenty of work to do even though I had a little time to do it. I want to be a simple Teacher again; I want my life back because I was not cut off from life.

Ngingumlomo ongathethi manga! My family was scorned as I was scorned. If I had to stay behind bars any longer, my mind would have exploded into the tiniest pieces and never to be put back together again because my first night in Prison was a hight of living hell. I do not say that lightly. I wish all men's time were the same and none had more pain than any other.

Anticipation of death is worse than death itself. The truth hurts. Well! No man is an island as the Parole Board members were some of the people who offered some hope to me but I judge it a mistake to place my hopes too high because my so-called "Enemies" are not people who deal in bluff, they advance step by delicate step with every plan laid and the ground ahead tested. They must therefore know something,

something to their advantage but some astonishment is at hand. I had chosen that way of bringing it out into the open as I am not one to hold my tongue on injustice.

Parole Board Conference Hall is a good place to talk and listen. It seems appropriate to feel paranoid about everything because the large Conference Hall seemed forbidding at that hour. Surely, I impressed the Parole Board Members that I wanted to co-operate in any way that I could as I was always praying that someone will be sent to listen to the side of my story.

Now that I am away from the Parole Board at Kroonstad Correctional Centre, my latent feelings of doubt rose again. I am more confused about the whole issue of Criminal Record; SACE and the question of how I would retain my reputation when retaining my position as a Teacher again. They had advised me to go to the Clerk of the Court after my release from Prison, to fill in the forms of cancelling my Criminal Record so as to deal with SACE in any way as I could because they themselves can't help me in that regard and they indicated that they know nothing about Department of Education Policy.

Things seem different when you have weighed the good and the bad hence, I had an inkling of fear. The thought that it may be nuts to force a confrontation with the Clerk of the Court as well as SACE, but I decided to press on because for me, this fear is called Counterphobia.

In my opinion, looks can be deceiving hence her skeleton is out and in the open as her performance on that specific day was out of this world but life is too short to hold grudges as we all have our vices hence everything has its own time. Ahmed Kathrada once said: "The hardest thing to open is a closed mind."

The truth has little to do with the human logic system because God does not create in Black and White. For the first time in so long I believe, and I love the feeling. Dear Lord, please give me a sign because I feel protected by someone or something unseen. Someone or Something who loves me.

I wish to soften the moment; to make it less dramatic; less harsh. I could only do it in my own gentle fashion even if it has been years; months and days of sadness and surprises. Some people were right in what they said and what they hinted but they were not strong enough arguments hence they were children as a result my so-called "Enemies" could scarcely bear the thought of facing the polite world with their hideous secret which is ready to be betrayed by a chance word .

The question is: When this is over, would my old self re -appear? God only knows.
I have decided to have a strange image of myself; to be very open; very free and easy and yet hold myself off from people. I have learnt that, there are certain

subjects which one does not discuss openly, even when one is in liquor therefore I will not take Beer with an enemy or stranger if we were the last two people left on earth.

I slept on my decision hence new dunghill and new cockerel to crow.

Treat me as anything less and it will be worse for you. Even it is said, bitterness will be wasteful but destructive can profit me nothing at all.
I was like Taurus, the stupid patient bull whereas they were like Sagittarius, the Archer who shoots me between the shoulders - blades while I was looking elsewhere.

I am a man who might be led to something but cannot be commanded. I do not judge at all. I accept what has happened but certainly I will make my own terms in the future hence I feel a swift return of my confidence.

The woman alone is enough to put God's curse on any place, time, and day. This made me realise that I was drugged by love to wrong women with beauty which delighted me by day and tormented me in mighty dreams. It was their breasts which my eyes searched when I talked with them. All because they had a pair of breasts, fit to blind a man's eyesight and they blinded mine too.

It was their gentle form; voices and their softness which had been tormenting me or placing me at a distance for the reason of feminine strategy. We had been friends in the good and bad days; we use to preserve peace and keep the pattern of friendship. We were strong and loving but we were not united.

I am still wondering what I can make of it and what it might make of me but I must ground here and take my chance of what is in store for me because a man is bound to know more than one woman even though this is just like a nest of Criminals which could not be flushed out .

Nobody knew what was happening to me. I did not know what was happening to me. Whether I had been tricked into agreement or cajoled or threatened. It did not matter a jot because I believe that, tomorrow would bring back all the things which are finest fabric of my life of which are: adventures at Prison, fighting; danger and freedom. I would then squeeze accounts with my so-called "Foes" and earn my due from them which is "Respect."

They will turn tail and run at first conviction because the proud so-called "Victim or Complainant" had already become the troubled child. This is the person who would have sold me into death. She deserves the same fate and she and her little team are within an ace of earning it. The Sun must have melted my brain, but defeat might be spitting in their very faces.

If that seemed to make me a Coward then I am a Coward, a live and prudent Coward with other work to do and other battles to win. Only time and chance could bring me the advantage. In the meantime, there is more profitable employment than plotting and scheming to square accounts with an enemy who in almost all circumstances could laugh at my efforts.

Beastly Bosses have shaved years off my life and then defended themselves as some of the most gifted people I've known. For me, there is no justification for jerks in the workplace. Titles are only Title because they can honour a great man or disguise a small one, even fools can sometimes talk sense.

Have no fear, I am paid because I was like a culprit summoned to account for the so-called "Misdeeds" which reflected to them as "Unnatural Sexual Offence." My attendance at their hearings was of less consequence and they falsely and unfairly regarded me as an example of "Bad Teacher" who was there to collect his pay.

The man in authority summoned me, no to punish but to warn. Hatred darted out of their eyes like a snake's tongue. It was therefore a time I did not give way to fooling anger because I knew if I succeeded, they would have drunk my blood. From that day of my conviction I saw no more of them as I was kept and locked in a God's forsaken hole by a man with authority in every word and gesture.

Inside there I therefore got enough time for thinking, not for fighting and I began to see that some of the inmates like myself were and still are as Victims as much as the so-called "Complainants." I also realised that there is more to life than fighting and hatred because for me, death is the only stage on our journey that is all we need to know. I believe, it is alright to cry, and it is bad to suffer in silence and repressing emotions.

You blurt. You deny. You apologize but one man is set apart to be the Ruler and all other human beings in his or her kingdom have been born only to obey. Any man who challenges his or her rule must never be given a second chance to do so but he or she must be destroyed. Destroyed in circumstances which would serve as an example to anyone else who might have a like ambition. His or Her greatest trick like President Robert Gabriel Mugabe of Zimbabwe is to make sure people fear him more than they hate him and hate themselves most of all.

I believe that, *konke okwenzekile empilweni yami kungenxa yecebo likaMdali. Hhayi ngenxa yami.* Well! It is easy to make Religion the scapegoat for all the ills in society but blaming Religion does not resolve conflicts. I never hurt anybody. That honest is and true but there are those that give their minds to live upon another is due.

In our so-called Democratic Country – Mnandini, such news travel miraculously on invisible wings. Stories seem able to grow feathers and take flight; spanning Oceans; penetrating jungles; reaching aliens and friendly ears in the same whispered breath but I do not change with the watch. I endure forever and sustain myself hence I should keep them under close survey.

I have earned loyalty because I have moved with times and summoned in cursing all the devils in hell. I know what is in their minds, but they do not know what is in mine. If they thought ill of me, it would be silence, the most ominous silence in the world hence people smile at me because you smile at me.

Did you know that all trees have souls? When the forests are cut down, the wood – cutters always leave a few strong trees standing for the expelled spirit to live in. Otherwise they would be condemned to wonder the bare earth forever and hopeless without a home.

Men can come to God in different hats hence I was not in the mood for long faces and gloomy words. Everybody alive trusts hope because hope spiritualizes the earth. Hope is partly made of tears as well as smiles. It makes amends to humans for the swarm of ugly troubles which are destined to be let loose among us, and hope makes it always new.

It will be my endeavour to send my so-called "Enemies" a gift in return. They would perhaps want me to convey my thanks in person because people will not follow someone, they cannot see that is the ghost of a man who has forgotten them.

CHAPTER 27

CAN I SPEAK MY MIND?

In this toy Institution I had become something of a toy myself because it is said, I had overstepped convention and law even though my motives had been pure enough but that would weigh nothing with them. In truth, our country - Mnandini is beautiful, whether it changes or not. If I have you, I have everything. I can only be strong if you are strong.

I am bidden here for two purposes these days. I must find my enemy first; make certain of his or her position and strength; muster my forces then work to destroy him or her. To be a fearful bearer of fearful news though my patience is not far from its end. The worst is over.

The enemy has lost the momentum of treacherous surprise hence aimless slaughter of people who could be nothing except innocent. The witnesses are innocent because they knew nothing, and they saw nothing. I will have to find truth from them because the Government Officials found it difficult in deciding in a fair manner, who was the Swindler and who was the honest person because no one could bear witness to the punishment of another.

The tide had turned hence sword for sword; wound for wound. Whoever questions my authority, questions him or her. Hold your tongue! I will fall where I stand. If I am to die, I will take them with me because one grows tired of perfection. For me, promise is a fine dog, but performance is a better one thus better than never.

Am I to back away like a dog kicked in the muzzle? Should I lay down on my bed as quietly as a dog curling up for sleep? Who could be happy even in

Paradise when ill - starred suffering is also near enough to be touched; loud enough to be heard and vivid enough to be felt?

My so-called “Enemies” have kept their oath. They enjoy their conquest to hate me for what I had not done and for what it might do in the future but it is another matter altogether to carry this hatred over to the realm of peace and having me at one’s mercy and to take pleasure in my prolonged punishment. They forgot that the blackness could not hide anything from any eye which is privy to such shame.

They had done enough harm already and must be content to watch the reaping of the vicious harvest they had sown. To be imprisoned; lost my job and reputation did good to them and that is more than all the sum of what is happening currently.

How could I have guessed this hideous outcome for a calculated plotting? I had endured nearly five years of questioning and probing insults as well as threats , I was wearied to death of it hence there was a temptation to say: "I did it and I am glad of it, now do your worst " but I couldn't quite bring myself to such a point of defence because too much was at stake. I had my occupation; reputation; family ... to lose as a result, I had to defend everything even if I had stood alone, I would not have delivered myself over to their malice.

Do I have to say a thing ten times before it becomes clear? Well! I am not afraid of names and labels because I believe that a family that prays together stays together. Those who still choose to fight are cornered and subdued because I kept them at a long arm's length as their evil deed is the nest which must be wiped out.

Nothing was turning out according to my forecast because they returned uniform answers to all questions as they were having keener nose for a reward. I had to take the hazard of their deeds on my own shoulders because I could never stand in the way of their serious planning of which all trails had run dead like river trickling into sand.

It is not a matter of piety. It is a question of reputation. If it goes badly, everything I value will lie open to the enemy. If I fail, then my family will perish like fruit withering on the vine. Victory would be the great salve for such troubles because it will be victory which will bind up all wounds and ease all pains. I will have to gamble and hopefully it will be worth it, and they will not point a finger on me.

I have seen my loophole and my advantage therefore I had to act upon it because all their actions and words give no hint of what is real and what is a dream. As a result, they will jump as if they are feeling a flash across their backs.

I am thinking a little of the past and a great deal of the future because I was falsely imprisoned, and my occupation is gone. I would have recalled my words if I could, for I loved them to inflict such careless wounds but I couldn't recall my mood which remains constant in its mixture of boredom and frustration because one is inclined to suffer when someone personally known is to make a public appearance.

I took it upon my own conscience. I told no one what I am planning because I believe that, even skeleton survival might be sweeter than death. For me, it is the gross idea of killing time again as if man should be satisfied to squander the Heavenly gift of life on the sweet nothings; waiting to be plucked from the languorous air. Holding my head high amid these pinpricks even though I was sometimes beginning to have doubts of my own, but I am always praying for success.

The war is over. It is won. Now I have nothing to fear even though I am conscious of delicate and dangerous ground as there are men who can grow to be giants if need be , in order to fulfil their destiny, otherwise they will not receive more honours than one man can safely bear.

As Prisoners, we were shackled together in droves of two and I was always asking myself some riddles like, why am I here? Why should I stay? What is in the future? What fate rules me? None of these riddles helped me to divine the future instead they cloud them almost beyond discovery, but fresh air is the best ointment for the wound.

Maybe my thoughts are too much for my tongue. Forgive me for intruding on your privacy because I thought my place is to be by you, bringing home victory and not going to a funeral. No word of regret or remorse; no plea for mercy had crossed my lips and my spirit will never mend with all these sour looks on it. If they have spies, then I must have spies of my own and no man shall die until he or she has learned his or her lesson.

When National duty calls, you answer even though some things are more important than business. I was my Employer's favourite and now I have lost favour. The peace and happiness which I had hoped for seemed to be receding rather than drawing nearer. I wasted my time and my wits because I have proved my innocence times without number and my appeals should have melt their stony hearts but they cursed and upbraided colleagues for their interference because they felt and thought that , they were about to be robbed of their pleasure and their prey - who is me.

At one time, they were happy to lean on me. At another, they were jealous of what I have become and of what they have made me. They became greedy and determined and they also never forget the point where their plot will fester and ripen and burst out. It is an old score which I must pay off hence I blocked my ears.

The so-called "Complainants" were or are like dolls jerked by a string and I am after bigger game - the biggest of all. The man whose hand is on the string has become worse and I have become better. They then put their heads together with another dark and faceless enemy as a result, I was left to salve the wound to my self -esteem as best I could hence I am a Captain without a ship, a fighter without an enemy.

We are not living in some sleepy ; comfortable world especially here at Ebumnandini because the bedevilled scene of fear is still here for instance, An Assistant Teacher like myself remains a subject of all the so-called Principals; Managers or Employers - high and low and do as they are bidden. If they do not, they pay for their disobedience by being dismissed from their jobs as a result I feel so strong that I am ready to take all this blame.

I was not born to sit in the Sun, doing nothing hence there are times when I feel myself growing older by the hour with nothing done and nothing to show for all the years going by, therefore as a man I need not sit idle unless I choose to.

When the time is ripe, all doubts and puzzlements will melt away. When their mood swings like a weather cock and rage gives way to brooding doubt and the restless muttering like a wind stirring dry leaves, then I will turn such thoughts to ashes and thereafter wishes them long life. My family was miserable when I was away all because of that learner -girl who is sly as a fox and dangerous than electricity. My family became happy on my return. My beloved wife is the most loving woman in the whole world, someone to continue my legacy. My family welcomed me as the glove welcomes the hand. In my opinion, talk and drinking is cheap, it does no harm and modesty is a matter of behaviour, it needs no clothes to aid it.

CHAPTER 28

WHAT CAN BE DONE?

I hope when you begin, you will not wish to stop reading. Read, Read, and Read with an open mind.

The whole place has sprouted ears and eyes. It seems as if I am losing friends too, every day. I am always wondering at the foolish way in which gossip could twist and turn and stretch the truth beyond proper shadow of its proper shape. I could not leave for better or for worse. I had no home in all the world, save Intabanhle and Esibayeni in Umhlola - Ekukhanyeni. My place is here, and it will remain here. I am bound to my beloved family; honest friends and colleagues and especially my love of life - a true flower of Mazibuko Clan, who might wither and die if she were to be transplanted.

All that remained of that time at work were rueful questions like, what had happened to those golden days of hope? Was it simple jealousy; an old onset of spite and fear so deep rooted that nothing could now dissolve it? It seems that my so-called Employer was in the thick of this matter and he will stay in the thick of it.

The ridiculous charges: the phrases set in isolation and the trusting of words had indeed been skilfully marshalled in a sense. The conspiracy of silence had been completed. I could only brood on the danger and evil which is in the very air, even in this private corner of our world.

The purest love turning to the purest hatred and yearning to rejection. Whatever drives me to try to withstand evil is the fact that, men are not fools nor knaves. They are born with love but sometimes lose it on the journey. If pressed, they would answer harshness with the vilest cruelty, yet it need not be as the touchstone.

Forgive me, I feel strongly therefore I speak strongly because my so-called Employer and Umhlola Regional Court Magistrate would hear everything, but they would not hear a word. I am not only victim among their ill-will; indeed, I may be the least of them. Whether you believe it or not, of all things done right or wrong in and around Umhlola, one flower - the rarest will bloom to such delicate perfection.

The Innocent has nothing to fear and the Guilty one dies. No! I am innocent - I stand fast. They can fashion Phakama School into their own image; spoil it; destroy its true nature and call it their own but that is not holding it but that is raping it. If they hurt themselves, they would not do so again.

Cruelty and Fear have turned their wits hence a stop-gap friend whose friendship shed its worth in the space of which resulted to the re – unions lose them by and by and stakeholders dispersed. I was and still dealing with people of consequence who take such matters seriously. It may be that I am to be saved from mortal sin. The little that remained of an awesome night passed like some fearful dream moving past deadly hazards at a snail's pace.

In my disturbed mood, I scarcely noticed anything amiss. I might have made a compact with some mangy tiger prowling the edge of the jungle , seeking hyena's meat but the time for such nonsense has past and we could now move on to adult pastures because my thoughts are in danger of being exposed before they are fully ripe for the light of day . The blows of life seemed to have implanted a respectful humility because such people bore the worst reputation of all.

I had said my say and I might as well have left it unsaid. That is the way of the world because we had not laughed together for a long time even though laughter is the most blessed balm for all the cares in the world. In this musing, I had reached the point; the somewhat desperate point of wondering what I could do with the rest of my life and of knowing to save my face as well as my self - esteem. I therefore must devise some useful and innocent employment which would not provoke my ex - Employer's wrath.

We have been at each other's throat as a result I have lived to regret it in many ways as it was for me , a cleft through this chattering confusion like knife through cheese thus an ant - hill disturbed by a giant foot could not be thrown into a greater uproar . We are people, not pawns. Let them fight their own battles.

Europeans have a corrupting influence on simpler people. They may come with the best intentions, but they introduce unhealthy novelty; they change what should be left unchanged and they turn innocence into evil. If they hurry us, it is usually done for selfish motives of profit as a result, they are likely to destroy all that is good.

Let me jog your memory. The secret of good Government is to let men alone otherwise it would be contrary to the natural law hence so many and even innocent Inmates in Ebumnandini's Correctional Centres. I have tried to learn from this Community as well as to teach. I have tried to promote the best of our Customs and to curb the worst cruelty and corruption. I discovered that, it is easy to say one thing in the Community and never to hear the echo of what you say thousands of kilometres away.

I was in a workman - like apartment in which I found it difficult to pass the time and lacked exercise to keep trim. There was also whispering and moving behind its walls and shadows including inside. I was distressed beyond measure by the happenings of those fatal hours and listened in agony for the next blow to fall but I will not shrink from this worst stroke of all. Yes! I could feel home sick, but I did not make any move at that juncture but let other people make their moves.

The day began to go sour when I was unfairly dismissed from work and wrongfully arrested and imprisoned with no relevant concrete or circumstantial reasons but I am still alive with thought and with the search for hope because I am sick and tired of this play cat - and - mouse game by pocketing my pride. Look at them! Their eyes are darting from side to side as if seeking hidden enemies. They are not close; they are lifetime away hence they have done more harm than good. According to me, they deserve nothing but shame. In my understanding, back to back is the punishment for Unnatural Acts between men therefore who wields it, rules by fear.

There is some poison at work, if it cannot be cured, it will infect all of them and they will wake up to find that, they are as deep in cruelty and deceit as their predecessor who has risen highest of all. Hopefully, there he will stay. I could not blame the wicked man for imputing worse wickedness to himself. It made me realise that people are too afraid to do anything but to submit and suffer because they lack a leader.

Surely, I had failed in my task. If as it seems, I cannot teach children, at least I can teach. Though I could not bring back the past even if I truly wanted to, there is no great harm occasionally in sighing for it. I earnestly pray God that, the right Teacher and Servant may be guided to this unhappy land and not someone who will plunder nor enjoy hie or her leisure but to teach; to serve and to liberate.

God's work in this land is enshrined in the two words which are Instruction and Love. Love must take place of oppression and duplicity. Only if love be armed and girded for combat. All is forgiven! I bring only sweetness and light. My candle will burn bright and upright in this naughty world especially here in Ebumnandini because at certain cross – roads the time for action is also time for truth.

My attention could perfectly well be in two places at once hence I had great dreams, but the dreams are lucid also, founded on fact and probability and are the fragile web of speculation. I am the man of large hopes who had been awaiting my chance to transform them into action because Soldiers prefer a strong Ruler – an armed man who knows his or her own destiny.

I could play this game of patience with the best player in the world hence I will not beg for friends in and around Umhlola because they are trying to slander me before the whole country – Ebumnandini. I do not have to because I will find others and I have already found them as I was enjoying the company of the so-called Inmates without reservation as we shared our thoughts and found in them a matching delight.

They are people whom I had only heard of, by repute as rascals and swindlers but I discovered them to be very reverse; witty; subtle and good hearted. When I was talking and questioning, they loiter nearby to hear what I had to say on any matter under the Sun because between myself and them, anything and everything was and still is meat for hopeful speculation.

We are currently trying to estimate the future position and strike one kind of balance thenceforth each plan leads to another; each idea has its lively offspring and its footbridge in to the future hence I have decided to open a 54.0 Parole Enterprise in future even though I will be opening it to friends as well as enemies too, thus a wise Commander deploys his or her Allies first.

I strongly believe that the Parole Board Members who asked for my audience on the 04th of August 2016 in Kroonstad Correctional Centre might have been sent by Providence in direct answer to my discontent.

They also made me realise that, to learn is to jump into the deep end.

If anyone is willing to be my audience, I am ready to give it; to find out and what his or her business is all about so that we could also find something to turn our hands to and to wander around at will.

I learnt that, Poison is the weapon of Cowards and of love - sick women. I had risen, perhaps I had fallen but I am still a man who believes that, in poor places, Heavenly flowers grows. Thus, every need of man from his or her need of a full belly to his or her need for God.

Thanks be to God and to my beloved wife who made me realise that there are no problems which could not be solved as I was feeling foolish and guilty at the same moment.

My lovely beautiful wife with whom I had joined my life, lay everything a man could desire and more than he could deserve. Nothing can mar our happiness and no force in the world can take that away from us hence a new child comes with a new beginning. We men take our pleasure in women; we wear them out with labour, and we kill them with talking as a result I fear the future as much as my wife.

Let me tell you a story of Cupid and Psyche. Once there lived a King who had three beautiful daughters. The fairest of them was Psyche who was also the youngest. Venus, goddess of love and beauty became jealous of the young Princess and sent her Son - Cupid, god of love to make Psyche fall in love with some wretched creature on earth.

Cupid took with him two Urns. One filled with sweet water and the other filled with bitter fluid from the magic fountain from his mother's garden. He found Psyche asleep in the Palace. Bending over her, he sprinkled the waters of bitterness on her lips. He touched her with the tip of his arrow which would make her fall in love.

Startled by the pain of the wound, the Princess awoke but could see no one, for the god was invisible to mortal eyes. Cupid, alarmed by her awakening, accidentally cut himself with the arrow he was holding and immediately fell deeply in love with Psyche. Before flying away, he emptied the water of sweetness over her hair. Two elder Princesses were wooed and married noble Princes Psyche was so lovely, but none sought her hand. Her parents, fearing that they had offended the gods who were thus punishing them by effusing Psyche a husband, consulted the Oracle of Apollo. The Priest told them that, they were to lead their youngest Daughter to the Peak of a Lofty Mountain. Here they would find a dreadful winged Monster whom even gods feared - he was to be Psyche's husband.

Here, she was found by Zephyrus – the gentle West Wind, who gathered her in his arms and carry her over the mountains, laid her on a mossy bank in a beautiful Valley where she sank into a deep sleep.

On awakening next morning, Psyche saw a grove of stately trees beyond which stood a magnificent palace. The massive front door stood open and soft voices bade her to enter. She entered the vast Hall, and she found a perfumed bath prepared for her and her refreshed herself in the sweet water.

Wo He! If you are interested to hear the whole story do some of your own research and I believe you'll get it because when the heart swelled with gladness at the beautiful sound, my heart is touched with the sweetness of thy music.

Oh! Perfect Beetle circling dung. In perfection egg begun.

Oh! Perfect Bee and perfect flower. Ritual perfect hour.
Oh! Perfect Web and perfect Fly. What a perfect way to die.
With this Poem, I refer to spider, fly, beetle, and bee, then you can decide what it means to your life and other people's lives.
Women are lovely and innocent as a snow leopard, even when they rend, they are just as dangerous to me. I am not a man for divided loyalties. When I had a woman, I stuck with her.

Money is money. Men are men. If they have told me I was having an affair with a goal , they might have something to talk about but the message is clear, compete or die hence the game is still the best game in town as they are like mosquitoes sucking blood of people. The way they spoke reflected the way they live hence they were under my skin like a barbed dart.

When you tell the truth, at least you expect sympathy, but they made me feel like a baby. They never listened to me, but they have nothing to win and I have everything to lose and they get off scot - free whilst I look like bad news.

Sad bones in the closet and dead cat on the creep! If I had me a pistol, I had put me to sleep. If I were to touch her, I should know the fire of all hells.
Hell is real hence someone had to straighten her out and I am good at things like that. This is only the beginning; I shall meet them again. I am sick of the whole thing because a part of mine is fading away like a whisper, forgotten in the wind.

CHAPTER 29

TRUTH CAN'T HARM ANYONE BUT A LIAR

Why do I keep saying Blacks this and Blacks that? It lives me breathless to be raised under White rule. Blacks raised under Whites are free to look around and wonder at the nonsense of any tradition, any rule or custom. Whites gave a Black child a fresh start with no tradition to follow; no ancient burden to carry and no family to impose goals. I am alone but free.

I do not believe in the rules that the Blacks impose on themselves or the rules that the White people impose on the Blacks, but I believe that they believe. Their delusions blacken their hearts. Whites wise God I believe is a lover of blood. In the Name of the Lamb – Christ, the Whites or Europeans have subjected whole people; erased cultures because they are primitive people who pillage the soul; who banish ideas; who rape the earth of her treasures and they spoil the beauty of their own lives as they steal it from others.

The Whites passed laws in our own Continent – Africa against coming of the wives because, with the wives would come breeding and breeding would create more foreign people therefore we are judged with Western heart. Our Black thoughts are so strong, held for so long and they have become real, real enough to affect even the unbelievers so that we must live in the black world they have created for us all because one or two cannot change what the multitude has decreed.

Let me cite an example, who had we decided cautiously and carefully to groom and support in his or her future bid for the Presidency of Ebumnandini? Better to test the water before diving in - one way or the other. The truth never reached the depths of the mind, but the truth is deep enough.

Without hate, love dies and being an old hand at something does not make it legal. It seems, all I ever done and all I ever said leads me to this bare room with an empty bed. Today, there is no better way to start than to cultivate friendship in high places therefore it was not fishy, but it was fixed. We must nip it in the bud otherwise it would be another big feather in its cap.

Stroke a banker, win a bank! You learn something every day if you listen. For instance, in China, marriage is not the result of romance, but it is an economic necessity. Most of them are paired at birth because to them marriage forms strong Clans and father healthy children. If a wife is unfaithful and worse by conceiving, the whole Clan suffers because bloodline is confused but if the man is unfaithful of which there is no such concept in marriage in China, why should the wife feel jealous or threatened?

She had her home, her children, and her marriage status. In China, the woman rules the home, and the home rules the Chinese – ultimately the woman rules as she does everywhere. It is only the Western African man who does not recognize this.

In Ebumnandini, America … a wife gets upset if her husband sleeps around because to them marriage is rather personal as a result the wife feels personally betrayed. In China, husbands should be as Heaven to their wives, wives as slaves to their husbands because what a man does outside a wife's bed is not a wife's business but what a woman does is quite the opposite. It is said, in China, adultery is only a feminine vice.

I believe, any issue that does not cause a Reader to rise out of his or her chair and cry: "Great God!" is a failure.

What I experienced in my life made me realise that people do not dodge trouble, but they make it. I am presently not wanted at Schools and stopped being wanted when I stopped being useful. She got me in, and she would pluck me out when their plan blew inside out in their minds like an umbrella in a high wind.

I learnt that, if you make a stupid law and you will get a bunch of law-breaking Citizens. Once they break one law, they find it easy to break another.

Why is it a crime for a woman to use her own body any way she pleases? Why is it a crime to sell alcohol to millions who wants to buy the stuff?

The Officials draw their power from laws, the people from the secret Societies. It took me years to figure it out, but it had finally dawned on me for what, where and who is what?

When I know more, people shall know more about the dirty deeds and shady deals but none of them will touch me. The cops were paid to leave them alone and keep their mouths shut but whatever they could do, I could easily counter. Nobody can tell what is good and what is bad anymore because for certain favoured people especially women, Police turn a blind eye which resulted to more law to be broken.

Wanting is not doing, sometimes people must trust their instincts hence I am not afraid of anything physical. Everything that scares me, I carry around with me on the inside. People must not ask forgiveness for what is naturally to them.

No more pussy - footing around with the niceties. I want to get this over as fast as it takes me to piss because what they accused me of , was over before it began but they made sure I stayed bottled so that it could take me years to get back on the road hence they dropped me like a hot cake - knife .

We need to know. I need to know otherwise what the hell am I doing? I would never get over it until I have paid them back to expose whoever is the brain behind whatever she does. Things are now moving like I wanted them to move of which next time was sooner than they thought. For me, manners are a dying art hence I feel no remorse nor pride. It is just wheels within wheels because, I am new to them and had just entered the circle.

I have more than sand against them for their crimes which are against ideas and values and a man's dreams. They are first -class criminals and public enemies. Being dumb is not always being cute because they are not trying to protect them, but they are trying to protect themselves in pretext of the natural protective response of the male towards the female. They have been toying with me. It is the snuffing out of a candle, the closing of a music box. The flame and music are gone but this is the game that they shall both lose because they are on real shaky ground.

Politicians change like Seasons hence a possible Ebumnandini President in the pocket could be better

than gold and I would last forever because words last through time and action fades like a smile.
I am beginning to feel like myself again because such things like revenge have a way of backfiring hence the air got suddenly thin because some games play with rough rules as they got to her with their silver tongues. Maybe you and I must not be on the same side hence she had gone into hiding.
You can't judge a book by its cover but today men are judges by the cut of their clothes; the pattern of their speech; the School they attended ; their wealth ; their wives ; by anything and everything . I believe that a nan can choose life for himself. Where I come from, a Whore is a Whore; a Thief is a Thief; a White is a White and a Bitch is a Bitch. Maybe where you come from, a Whore can be a Debutante; Thief can be a President; White is a dead man, and a Bitch can be a rude broad in a stupid hat.

I have looks and brains as well as the sense to use them – it was no accident hence I discovered that, there are two types of men, those who went and those who did not. If a man is in the book, that is who he is. If he is not, who is he? White girls do not live with Black boys. If they found life on Mars, White girls would not live with those boys either, but the boys get strong up their balls.

Why does beauty give pain? Is it because all beauty dies or because it lies? It cannot be held and cannot be possessed hence for me, it is fortunate to meet a friend and most unfortunate to meet a pretty woman because a woman either finds herself in one world or the other thus there is no crossover .Man, on the other hand is forgiven for his weakness because the state of man is to be weak but a woman is never forgiven because a woman's lot is strength. Being strong at what she does, she is solely responsible.

Why are you of all people doing this to me? Is it because of one true twin - headed religion - Money and Democracy? To tell the truth I have not the faintest idea who will benefit most. I hope that it will be you. Any loyalty that I had felt towards you had evaporated like boiled sake because you live in a world of her own creation. You must make a choice because having chosen could never go back. You and I have gone a journey that can end in nothing but tragedy.

Habits once formed die hard. It had happened before, and it would happen again. A man of means and breeding can get away with anything because people only fought where there was something to fight for. It was all for the best.

Hearing things and proving things are not the same hence there have been all sorts of rumours flying around. I've seen too much to even be surprised as a result I had nothing to fear from fate. I would neither seek it nor would I avoid it. Nothing was getting said, nothing asked.

In my opinion, the Government is human just like people because Business operating is not for the Community but for themselves. See no tricks when the truth began to leak out because when the trouble comes to a man, it wore cleats.

Discipline begins with fear of death. When a dragon is stranded in shallow waters, all the shrimps laugh. People can yell their heads off but a wise man in a fool's service is like a pearl dropped in lacquer. If you want to be like a human, you should act like human. Maybe I was not good enough for a dog. I know all these because I did a lot of dumb things when I was younger too.

People think if they are rich, everything would be smooth as a baby's butt, but it is not like that at all because money blurs the edges of things therefore choices are not obvious. I'd rather spent hours reading about everything else because something long dormant in my mind is struggling to wake – a critical sense; judgement; curiosity or whatever it is.

Spending a year and six months behind bars is all I got because they have won, and it is not going to change their evil deeds because the Psychopaths are wondering loose around the streets. Well! I was not afraid I would fail to win but I was afraid of what I might get myself into when I succeeded to save my own neck and not to put the finger on anyone. We all must learn the hard way because being human means to go out and take the licks coming to you and then learn and recognize opportunity when it smacks you in the face.

I have shut that last of my ex- learner's files because the memory is like catching on a fleeing dream in daylight as a result, I must take a dive. The Student teaches the doubting Master because, my imprisonment has taught me many things and my pride kept them unprepared. So now I must do more.

This is a Newspaper! Isn't it? We need all the lies we can get. My sight made the headlines not black but red because my so-called "Case" was not as open and shut as the Newspaper would and anyone would have believed. The Police and Prosecutors have been too hasty of getting me as a result people shunned me as if I were toxic with exotic disease. I can assure you that, the devil does not come calling twice or does he or she? The way I play the game, patience is everything. If a man has fallen down a well, there is no need to stone him or her.

What begins with a dragon's head often ends with a snake's tail hence on the final day, her tongue was not only silver but platinum. She has got only herself to blame, it is her stew as she chopped up all the Onions. No wonder she has got to be the one doing the crying.

The more I heard that, she was to be soothed; smoothed and wooed, the worst it got. My heart was leaping about in my chest; the palms of my hands were wet, and I had to divert the heart since they had run out of Cards because They had played them all. Therefore, I have new heights to climb and getting out in time takes talent, but I do not know the right bait to catch a ringleader.

In my understanding, troubles test us because without them we would be like jelly fish with no backbone. You spit out that mess on me, I will make you eat it because my bite is much worse than my bark.

Being what they are, it is wiser to stick the evil deed to them before they stick it on to me because all Politicians owes favours as it happens in Business all over this country but one little mistake and he or she got the whole world on his or her ass. Their friends want to work with people they know hence our country's current President is so weak-willed and weak- minded but he was not a crook.

What a circus the world has become and I had my nose right in it because my ex- learner, the so-called "Victim or Complainant" wanted me to want it because these days women devours men and most women have go- to- hell eyes and the men look willing. I personally do not want what someone else wants because wanting things like that is a big mistake.

A man learns or a man dies but most of us men are easy as some of us like women who are hot and some like them cold. I fully agree with the saying: "When fishing for treasure in the Sea, be careful not to pull girls, there is no profit in raising girls. "Because nowadays, their eyes are clear and uncomplicated as water but deceiving and their eyes are eyes of a snake – flat; unforgiving and venomous.

They are striding than walking; their pride is like a second coating and no one gets close to them unless the price is right. My so-called "Victim" was only a part of the plan because of a dirty place and dirty people thenceforth she became the most popular girl in the township streets.

The girl I thought I knew became a pawn and a stupid temporary pawn at that. The year 2012 was a close shave, women being what they have become and me being who I am and sane. They wear what they want, and I wear what I want. When they do something, they do something therefore what do I want to fool around with that kind of grief for?

We were not cut out to be lovers, but she had the last word again and I stick to my guns. Does a tree or a girl or a woman fall if no one is looking or if no one knows? The people who believed them had made a few quite fatal miscalculations. Maybe it was because it was something unexpected and unthinkable, forgetting that it will be my neck on the block.

I have seen what I wanted to see and heard what I knew I will hear because even my sources told me that they were happy and that , if it goes further it may spoil my chance for the future. The only crime I had committed was to be at School when she arrives or maybe life ran out for her as a result, I was hounded; disgraced and became a scapegoat. What I realised is that the Prosecution had not convicted me, but my Employer did because when he speaks, he is listened to. He speaks a lot especially in Schools; Conferences; Funerals and wherever he is asked, which resulted to most people not to believe me.

Oh Gosh! The silly girl is making me look bad. Did she practice being a Bitch, or did it just come naturally? I guess she knew that tit for tat from the women is something men could not handle. Well! The game is the same. I just want to win as they did but currently, I am still at my drawing board chewing on my pencil stub because this is one of those times that calls for brains.

This is turning into a National Scandal. Heads are going to roll. She poured a jug of water – all of it into my bed in the middle of the night, with me still sleeping in it. When I woke up, I thought I had pissed myself until I found that she had been spying on me. I am talking about a very nervous egg that is about to get scrambled.

How could I forget? It was the worst day of my life. Christ! I will show them. Someday I will show them because they think they know what I am made of. They think otherwise! I will squeeze their hateful necks until their eyes pop out of their heads and cut then into red drippings … before skinning them alive.

I thought we were friends but we don\t want the same thing at all. At my age, this was the first crisis in our family sheltered life whilst they sit bold as beans on their Sofa and in their bloody high horse. What my family intended to create, I intend to nurture and they on the other hand will blow away like burnt paper in a hot wind thereafter I will step with my head high.

I made them look at things the way I looked at them and I made them laugh. I had waited; gambling on my charm and good looks to hold them without single or taking her out with my simple - minded purpose which was chilling but effective. I could handle that as easily as I could sum up a stacked murder case since there was no need to play rough. I fully agree that men who rape girls; women and grannies deserve what they got even if her crush on him was in full flower.

To be someone so socially unacceptable without knowing why? They had suddenly become the enemy. Together but not together. Place a bet! I am leaving them protesting to the thin air since I know what they think because it is written all over their faces. As for me, they are not ugly, but they are hideous by snooping on what other people are doing.

I had a lot to answer for, what did I do that day? How dare I took advantage of a girl – learner when she was not quiet herself? Is my family nothing but a decoration whose thoughts did not count? Did I, or Didn't I? There is one problem left and it is doozy which is, if anything had gone on between us, she must have started it – double demon. Did the Authorities and Officials ever consider the fact that, she had probably drove me to it but turned things around.

I am not a whole lot different from Sipho's or the Mandla's of the world. I have the same ambitions and the same methods. The only real difference lies in the size of my ambition and the scale of my methods. I had therefore lost the taste of women, replacing it with a taste for myself.

What a man truly loves, never dies, it just changes its tune hence men want women to act the way it makes them comfortable but not willing to learn the art of pleasing women. Men believe that, sleeping with women is the best way of controlling them which resulted in the belief that, their natural inclination is for action before thought. Be warned! Drinking alcohol over limit does not look good on men or women, not when the bottle is bigger than the drinker.

I know what I am doing, and I am doing it well. I am beginning to get the whole picture. Men find me manly whereas women find me delicious because I am highly visible. I want what I want and currently I am still doing what I do best - Teaching and Sports. If I do not count right now, the end of this war would be the worst thing that had ever happened to me.

I must have a lofty mind, perhaps even a visionary since I told people that things would get better and better. Men lives on their Names but I live on my nerves hence I will politely welcome hotshot Newspaper Reporters from Uzalo News and Umphakathi News about lies they published about me which has cost me so much especially my life and my mind is currently like a high wire act . What they have published about me was very quiet and very wrong hence people stuck to them like tar and fierce in their loyalty.

When has the colour of a man's skin changed his or her Soul? Greed belongs to us all but if they do not hold their horses, they will be emerging like rats from a Cellar, trying to get out at the same time and I will be the one to chant our descent line and blow away demons in the night. I was fighting with crocodiles whilst inside water since we were like water and wine. This aren't a news story, and I am not a reporter.

I am not thinking about the past. The future is the only kind of time that holds any interest for me - the future I am going to shape. Why back the tide? If I am doing it, I might as well get it right. I had had few girlfriends but who needs girls when one girl has all the boys?

Things looks like they looked because I have no eye for beauty and eye for the hideous either. Take it or leave it! I discovered that, she learned the ropes and paid with her body to get what she wants in life. She knew hard times and hard men; she knew what it is not to have money and knew class when she saw it.

People would not tell me because some of them were in on the scam. They say, when a girl has no talent, she uses whatever talent she has as she has a nose for the right look since she makes men unbend like candles in a hot oven. As a result, my world fell apart and my dreams went up in smoke hence I got the score to settle with her that has waited for approximately five years of my life.

I have two choices, the first is to sink under; hide and become small. The second is to rise; to grow large too and big to be hurt. I choose to rise as there is nothing left to lose.

CHAPTER 30

SIMPLE MINDS, SIMPLE TASKS!

If I have no Teacher and no one to guide me then I will teach myself because a man can make the world his or her by vision and effort. A man who can ride a tiger never dismounts. Death is bigger than a Mountain but smaller than a hair. Death is both too big and too small. Why waste time searching for it? I will come when it is ready. Meanwhile I ride my tiger because I can.

What I have become is what I have made myself because I realised that, with simple values like honesty; hard work and deference to one's betters gets a man exactly nowhere at all. I believed that, if evil is cut off at the head, the body would die too but now I know better. If the head is chopped off, the body would sprout another and another. Well! I am a Talker, not a Writer.

Death leaves the living with unseen wounds and a hideous mute fear. Gone where? Is there somewhere to go? What use are tears? They sooth the living. As for me, a dead man is a dangerous man.

Life is like a spring dream, dying like going home. Life is like a dance of shadows. The body like a mask. Surely it can only be by dying that one sees through the shadowed dance, where death shines with a fierce white light. For me, death is life and life a quick step towards death hence surviving is worse than death.

My mind is way ahead of my body because the way I am thinking is the way I speak hence I have a heart like a lion and the medical Doctor told me to go to bed but he didn't say which bed. What does it take to make a man learn?

To most of us, rules are belief and belief is reality. Reality is all that keeps the demons of chaos chained. The nature of belief and reality is the same everywhere, but the rules change from place to place as the weather changes from one day to the next. I had one more item to add to all this mystery which is, put in the last nail by putting this country in criminal map because of her source of power and unlimited ambition.

Now they had and still have a very silent business partners who know what their limits are and what would they want in return for getting rid of me as a result my voice fell on deaf ears. The more I knew about them, the less I knew about them. Only my lovely wife is smarter than a whip in my world. I could trust her to the ends of the earth.

What is clear as rain to me seemed to be mud to other people? Even if I am regarded as a man with many so-called "bad habits", I would never bite the hand that feeds me. I have ambition but I am wise enough to keep it from showing with no opinions as a loyal Citizen because opinions are not an asset. I am tall enough to be imposing but not tall enough to intimidate. Maybe my teeth are not good. So, I rarely smile hence people mistook it for seriousness.

Watch and listen! But keep your mouth shut because women talk the feathers off a parrot as a result some men are nervous as a drop of water in hot fat and I was so busy feeling sorry for myself; spinning in my tight humiliated circle of fear and revenge.

Nothing has really changed in and around Umhlola except my heart. I held my breath as long as I could hold my breath since nothing bad could happen to me because when I am not breathing, I am not really alive and if I am not really alive , I am not really here as a result no one could hurt me , not even ghosts who shook the land of the living Black and White devils.

Whatever I think and whatever I do counts for a great deal in our Townships. Conversely whatever people think about anything adds to zero. I suggest, people should sober up; gather their wits and make the best of things as they are hence the beautiful and the damned. What hurt most is not my so-called "Victim", but it is what I thought of her since she'd never thought to ask me about me.

All the hustle and bustle of Ebumnandini's complicated system. The lies I heard from the important mouths of important people, but I pull no punches because I suddenly realised that the war had been the best time of my life - my war. If I could keep my head up, I would fit in and by keeping my head in more ways than one as she and her little team are a pain in my ass.

Time had been kind to my spirit as a result I discovered that, it is money that talks in this country

- Ebumnandini. Money is nothing but Freedom. What is anybody without money?

The only value the Ebumnandinans understand is value of money because greed today is called ambition and mean is careful. Where the world is going to, if Ebumnandini's favourite Good God - man's soccer ball" could be sold down the river for a few measly cents. Oh Gosh! The spirits of the mad could bite our souls and parasites to feed on the blood of the Gold - Seekers because for them possession does not matter. What matters is the party hence they have their fingers on everyone's pie. They are jealous; ashamed and angry. I say: "To hell, straight to hell in the back pocket of greed."

The questions are: Who is who? Who chaired the Committee to chase me out of School? Were Doctors in Town having their hands full to check DNA; Bruises; Trauma or state of Emotions of the so-called "Victim" on that specific day?

What a surprise! I am flattered! What did the member of Syndicate do with the swells? He was sniffing and sneezing, and his eyes watered as someone who has a perpetual cold. He even yawned at the oddest times since his hands were always moving whilst he was talking too much. Asking silly questions like, where do you pee? Wasn't it some sort of defence mechanism? WO –HE! Everyone knew and loved me or at least had heard of me and this what I was accused of, was mayhem.

Why are all clever ones so ugly? Is it because the opposite of love is not hating but indifference? These questions made me realise that, If you are named after something, then you become that thing for practical example "*Dieketseng di taba di le seko*" meaning, exaggerate news which do not exist. I therefore suggest that, Famous people doing famous things had to be careful when they have fun, they ought to think twice about who that have fun with and never to do it under the nose of ambition.

Thanks Sweetie, that's swell of you because the blind destructive anger is gone since my heart and soul is going where the music takes me, a private place that everyone in and around Umhlola could see; where they all wanted to go - somewhere warm and quiet; where poverty; the cold and killing white; black or red eyes could never reach me.

I am used to the off - hand way she talked to me, not even when I went to her with my knees and begging. I ran out of fingers for she wanted to be the centre of the Universe because they are up to her neck in plots.

You ask. You get! I do some useful for a change instead of hanging around all day long. I would be the driving force behind a Campaign to clean up Ekukhanyeni especially in and around Greater Umhlola and get rid of the puppet master behind the scenes. Once a bad apple is gone, the province; townships and the country at large would flower like the Garden of Eden. Oh! I remember in 1970s, one of those sweetest years when Intabanhle at Umhlola though it was young and had a good grip on things and half the Ekukhanyeni Province as usual was asleep.

Where were my so-called "Friends" when I needed them? They were drinking strong black coffee or cold beer out of a cup or glass big enough for a full-grown frog to paddle in, using saucers or empty can tins as an ashtray. Oh my God! There was really my beloved pretty wife and my family and few honest friends as well as colleagues only because in such condition people need love, care, and support. I felt out of place but welcomed as they were always in my corner.

There is strength in numbers but there is power in a man who knows himself. It is breathing what I could achieve on such slim support because most people believed that my so-called "Case" was as complicated as a Chinese box, but a kind of unquenchable optimism made me believe in myself. As a result of my strong belief in my Almighty God and in my Ancestors hence I could not understand what the black and white demons said to me. Therefore, my respect for my God and my Ancestors is blooming like a peach.

My Beloved deceased Parents, "Ma Their Souls rest in peace" had willed me a kind of Freedom. A certain integrity of mind; a pioneering spirit and an honest heart. There had not left behind rules to break but they had left me the strength to make some for myself. I felt alone and afraid of being alone and murmured under a blanket of dreams because our Ancestors are our link to reality hence today I have someone to lean on and she cooks like an Angel as a result I think the world of her.

When water ran out, I used sewerage and when the sewerage ran out, I used beer because I was penniless. Insurances turned their backs on my claims as did other people including even Schools. When things cool down, I will be getting out to pay respect to them. I cross my heart as my life nearly fell in like a house of Cards and faster than anybody can spit.

Each person is travelling through life as though he or she is in a Boat going down a River. Without the structure of the River bank, the water will flow in all directions. Note that, the banks of the River provide the limiting factors which guide the Boat and give it added power to go down the Stream. The Individual likewise is free to make his or her own choices but always there seem to be a frame of reference which limits and gives direction to choose.

Due to what I experienced in my life, I learnt that Feelings are manifestations of the needs and drives which compel us to act. Feelings are elusive and often uncontrollable. Feelings do not possess evaluation quality and they are not right or wrong. Feelings can be described as the road to the deeper levels of ideas and experiences which constitute the individual's core system hence a person's feelings are generated by his or her ideas or perception.

The Individual through the aid of his or her ego system is the Evaluator of his or her experience hence clarifying feelings leads to clarification of the ideas and experience underlying these feelings as a result , careful scrutiny of our feelings leads us to examine the motivating forces underlying these feelings . The word "Because" often leads us right to the core motive or experience and person's past experiences ; feelings and basic needs are the roots of his or her behaviour hence ideas possess truth or falsity therefore choose what you think is good . Choose and honour your choice. It is more of a plea than a request.

All these made me realise that, the more the Expert is consulted, the greater the feeling of helplessness and the greater the need for further advising because we entrust our faith in the "Expert" for instance, how to rear our children; love - making; budgeting and so on as a result we shy away from our culture of which we are personally responsible.

Many people beg Therapists or Counsellors to tell them how to live; what kind of person they should be and to relieve them of basic anxieties such as fear of non - being or death. In my understanding, the role of Therapists or Counsellors is to make positive suggestions to the people concerning where they might search to find "Answers" or "Grist" for their religious and philosophical mill.

The Therapeutic Psychologist's principal role on the other hand is to help people to classify their thinking and to discover feelings and thoughts regarding questions of values in their own personalities. They do not attempt consciously to influence a person's basic life values because their personal values and attitudes toward life influence their professional work as much as their skills and training. They are often put in a difficult position when the people expect more of them than help in gaining insight into themselves.

This indicates that , there is one solution to man's problem which is to face the truth; to acknowledge his or her fundamental aloneness and solitude in a Universe, indifferent to his or her fate and to recognize that there is no power transcending him or her which can solve his or her problems for him or her. If he or she faces the truth without panic, he or she will recognize that, there is no meaning to life except the meaning man gives his or her life by the unfolding of his or her powers and by living productively.

Yes! Mna lives in a confused human situation therefore he or she must face up to the incongruities in this human situation through his or her own powers. He or She must discover his or her own values within him or herself and lean heavily on consensus and cultural norms because his or her possibilities and troubles are largely of his or her own making.

Man, in his or her life has the dual and simultaneous presence of the good and the bad for example, he or she is said to be sinful and destructive, yet potentially virtuous and loving too. The problem is how to help the individual seek victory of the good over the evil.

A man cannot develop his or her full human potentialities unless he or she is truthful to him or herself; unless he or she is active and productive and unless he or she relaxes him or herself to others in the spirit of mutuality. Apparently he or she cannot grow if he or she consistently attributes all his or her own shortcomings to the deficiencies of others but he or she can grow in the true sense, only if he or she assumes responsibility for him or herself which is basically morality.

I have discovered that, the most common moral problems amongst people are sexual one which take the form of anxieties about homosexuality; promiscuity; infidelity; masturbation and exhibitionism. A second type concerns accuracy of reporting which involves occasional dishonesty and lying all the way to gross; deception and cheating.

Disturbing the property and personal rights of others is another area of morals that involves the occasional people. Disturbing other people's rights often creates guilt and anxiety when the acts are committed impulsively or under the influence of alcohol or narcotics.

This group includes the alcoholics, delinquents, Vagrants and drug Addicts of which their acts of hostility though directed against themselves are sometimes mainly expressed against others but most of the problems of the Psychopath involve some legal action against him or her because their feelings rather than their acts are the principal concern of the Therapeutic Psychologist.

I learnt that, a striking characteristic of a person going for help on moral problem is the feeling of guilt. Guilt can be described as a broad pervasive feeling of wrongfulness. This feeling is closely related to feelings of inadequacy and fears of failure. Even the person successful by the usual social standards often have such feelings. This type of normal or healthy guilt is an intimate condition of human life and may even perform protective functions for the individual and his or her Society for example, "I am not really doing what I should be doing, and I should be doing something better."

The other guilt is experienced as an acute emotional reaction to a specific behaviour such as breaking rules against lying; cheating an Associate or stealing property, may arouse strong subjective feeling of having done something reprehensible which can be described as guilt.

I discovered that, one is very much aware of having broken a Social rule, a Religious injunction or moral law. These feelings seem to be the characteristic of most Cultures in the form of awareness for instance, that one is being watched and will be held accountable for his or her acts thus feeling guilty for having hurt somebody's feelings as it was done to me.

I also discovered that, in the Analytic process, such a person will slowly recognize that behind his or her authoritarian sense of guilt is another feeling of guilt which stem from his or her voice and from his or her conscience in the human sense. He or She will recognize that his or her sin is against him or herself of which is the sin of letting his or her power to love to go to waste. The first step in analysing a person feeling guilty of leading a promiscuous life is to discover that he or she really feels afraid of being found out and criticized by his or her parents; by his or her wife or husband; by public opinion; by Church and by anyone who represents authority to him or her. Valid guilt is present when man realises that his or her relationship with God is not proper. This feeling is manifested by an awareness of anxiety or even dead.

Displaced guilt on the other hand is that feeling of guilt that is detached from the original idea and appears in the individual's awareness as a different idea such as remorse over small act or a haunting fear that he or she has done something reprehensible like injuring someone with his or her car.

Normal or healthy guilt in the mature adult becomes a feeling of having violated the integrity of the self-system; a feeling of self - hostility for not achieving the ideal of the self - image and the habit of obedience in the adult gives way to self - guidance based on a broad schemata of values that confer direction upon conduct.

As a mature adult I make more selective and rational responses to environmental demands according to my growing self-regarding attitudes hence I still feel the guilt but it is normal or healthy , which helps me to reduce the gap between actualised self-values and inappropriate behaviour .

I discovered in my research that, normal or healthy guilt is universal and is of three basic types of which are, guilt against one's self for not fulfilling one's potentialities; guilt against one's fellow man for not meeting my needs and lastly guilt against nature or

God and a feeling of separateness or alienation there from.

Neurotic guilt on the other side of a coin, is an unaccepted and repressed normal guilt. It is said. Therapy therefore assists the person to accept and face his or her neurotic guilt and to turn it into normal guilt thus therapy should water down; expunge or neutralize guilt entirely.

I discovered steps that should be followed for changing neurotic to normal guilt of which are , One , the Counsellor should help the people to admit what he or she has done to feel guilty ; Two, to become aware of the motives underlying his or her guilt feeling especially those of destruction and hatred; three, cut through the rationalization which implies taking responsibility for what one does; four, transform neurotic - unfaced repressed guilt to normal guilt by assisting people to see that it can be tolerated and constructive and that, Traumatic incidents can be desensitized so that the intense suffering associated with neurotic guilt can be minimized and understood.

I learnt that, over - developed conscience expresses itself in a paranoid delusion in which the person's guilt feelings to others whom he or she accuses of criticizing or blaming him or her. It is clearly indicated that, a related defence is the pharisaically self - righteous person who defends his or her guilt stoutly by means of a superior demeanour and condemnation of others.

Emotional disorder is type of moral problem emphasising personal responsibility for behaviour. The sickness concept of emotional disorders and troubles of a normal person are the states of irresponsibility; narcissism; dependency and extreme aggression of which are not one's own fault because the sickness view indicates that the person can hardly be blamed for his or her condition hence he or she can place the blame conveniently on parental behaviours or environmental deprivation or other factors outside his or her control or personal responsibility.

Perhaps Clergyman ; Pastors ; Preachers and so on , are also becoming too bedazzled by the sickness concept of personality disorder and with psychoanalytic explanations of human problems because personality has laws that go beyond psychological laws and are concerned with man's ideals as well as responsible behaviour . This resulted to Logotherapy which is a form of therapy devoted to discovering the central purpose and meaning of life so that people can make a choice.

Immoral behaviour on the other side of the coin is said to be that which destroys self - respect and heightens difficulties in interpersonal relationships. It is further said, moral decision and conduct are those which result in improving the capacity of people to work together with trust and understanding but immoral or wrong conduct is that which creates distrust and suspicion; produces withdrawal and a decline in self - respect.

In my understanding, man's love for man is rooted in God's love for man hence Religion is needed to give purpose and direction to behaviour on the other. In my opinion, the present belief should be used in such a way that, it would hasten man's recovery of healthy attitudes hence it came to my understanding that, learning from past experiences becomes blended with present experiences so that one's ethical sensitivity is sharpened and one's level of insight is deepened.

A positive self - regard is the most dependable route to moral behaviour. When a person trusts his or her innermost feelings about him or herself, he or she learns that such trust will help him or her to make the wiser decisions. When an individual perceives him or herself as behaving in a manner consistent with his or her picture of him or herself, he or she generally experiences feelings of adequacy security and worth but if he or she acts in a manner different from the way he or she defines him or herself, he or she experiences what is known as a threat and feels insecure; inadequate or worthless.

If he or she perceives no other alternative, he or she may defend him or herself against this threat or inconsistency via defence mechanism. When a person is not acting in accord with his or her self - concept; he or she is maladjusted in the sense that his or her awareness of threat and anxiety and his or her consequent defensiveness are high but there is great danger in thinking of the "Self" as a type of homunculus or man within a man having personal qualities.

One of the roles of counselling is facilitating the transformation of the blind; impulsive and infantile conscience into a mature value structure in the self - system. I realised that, to feel at home in this Universe; to be value as a person and to feel close to someone are deep personal needs. One of the appeals of membership in and identification with broad social; political and religious movements is the feeling of close belonging and of being important to a significant cause.

One group affiliation plays a significant part in developing feelings of relatedness because relatedness must involve a high degree of intimacy like close friendship; comradeship; work organisation and marriage. Marriage provides opportunity for the greatest satisfaction of the relatedness need because in marriage there is at least one other person who cares deeply about one's self.

Work provides further outlets for such feelings and it is a paradox in several respects. Though work offers relatedness satisfaction, it often gives an individual the feeling that, he or she is regarded as a "Marketable Product." Work results to the vicious circle of the individual gaining decreasing satisfaction from family life and increasing his or her searches for satisfaction from work. This circle can lead to the other signs of personality deterioration such as, alcoholism or infidelity. Business Executive or Professional man derives most satisfaction for his or her feelings of relatedness in his or her work. Frequently he obtains little satisfaction from or contribute little of him or herself to which is the familial situation. As a result, many men and women feel they must choose between their families and their work. The mature and well-functioning person in our Society must be able to both love and work in the proper balance because our satisfactions are closely tied to work I such a way that the prospect of no work or being paid not to work have anxious implications.

CHAPTER 31

SPEAK EASY

A writer has many pages in his or her book, but I have none. Let me by please! It has been a hard secret to bear because I was woozy, but my driving was okay even though I was shit - faced behind the wheel of a car. After an accident, I could still breathe. I could still swallow but I could not move or speak. As a result, someone started mouth - to - mouth Resuscitation. I am the bearer of the terrible news hence a spatter of raindrops saved for tears.

Everyone has a life philosophy, a lifestyle, a set of religious beliefs even though they are implicit and not consciously known or felt by us. I believe I am a creature of God responsible to God with the hope of reconciliation and reunion with God.

A significant problem for me is how to be my true self within the tragic framework and disorder of my society. I realised that, belief conflicts are the root of many people anxieties for instance, late adolescent problem of discovering that one's familiar belief brought along from childhood suddenly seem to deteriorate into a morass of confusion and disillusionment due to intellectual atmosphere of Naturalism; Rationalism; Scientism ; Humanism and many other "isms " that pose threat to my childhood belief structure.

Much of formal religion, as for me , is a form of illness itself because a Church traditionally has been a Community of people enhancing one another's growth but critics of current highly Institutionalized Churches feel that, this fellowship of persons has been lost. It is a mistake for a Minister to become too involved in Therapeutic counselling with people unless the question involved discovering answers to deep - seated but rather clear - cut, moral and spiritual problems.

One must not assume that other religious concern or psychological interpretation is the total solution to and explanation of man's problems. I therefore suggest that a means must be found in addition to formal religion to help people with feelings of disillusionment; depersonalisation; being unloved and abandoned and of being a "Thing." Unscrupulously manipulated by other people. In my opinion, Pastoral counselling and nono-theological oriented counselling is both concerned with helping suffering humanity.

Religion and Psychology complement each other because, Religion contributes to an understanding of the meaning and purpose in life and the significance of the same relationships whilst psychology contributes to an understanding of the nature of self and one's relationships with others. Both may contribute to me effective living.

The Vocational Rehabilitation Act of 1965 broadened the concept of rehabilitation to include any person who has been hurt by life which includes not only the physically and mentally handicapped but also the culturally deprived and the socially handicapped such as released prisoners.

The classical religious conception of conscience from the Western Christian point of view that , man is born with a rudimentary conscience is sharpened through religious training by means of the following rationale ; that God created man with a certain nature ; that man is obligated to live according to that nature and that God revealed how He wants us to behave . If man disobeys, he or she has made an offense against God hence he or she is estranged from God. The result is that he or she feels guilty. This feeling of guilt creates a need for God's forgiveness and ultimately brings him or her back to God.

I discovered that, Humanistic religion is centred on man and his or her strength. Man must develop his or her power of reason to understand him or herself, his or her relationship to his or her fellow man and his or her position in the Universe. He or She must recognize the truth, both regarding his or her limitations and his or her potentialities. He or She must develop his or her powers of love for others as well as for him or herself and experience the solidarity of all living beings. He or She must have principles and norms to guide him or her in this aim.

Religious experience in this kind of religion is the experience of oneness with all, based on one's relatedness to the world as it is grasped with thought and with love. Man's aim in humanistic religion is to achieve the greatest strength, not the greatest powerlessness and virtue is self - realisation not obedience.

In as much as humanistic religious are Theistic who believes God is a symbol of man's own powers which he or she tries to realise in his or her life and not a symbol of force and domination having power over men. Humanism believes that man alone in a morally neutral Universe and that man is in his or her own moral referent therefore man's troubles are believed to be of his or her own making. He or She is limited in his or her achievements by his or her nature.
Man's quandary is solved within him or herself by a process of reason and the methods of self - discovery involved in Psychotherapeutic methods such as psychoanalysis. There is a strong belief in man's powers of growth and positive motivation to solve his or her own and Society's problems. Conditions like death for example must be accepted as human fact with no necessary implications for further life.

The Christian view emphasises man's alienation from God and man's realisation of this estrangement results in much basic anxiety. Klann in a Symposium on Psychology and Christianity stated: "Man's anxiety is the product of his or her sinfulness, that state of alienation or contradiction which exists between him or her and God ; between man's will and God's will because man's being is derived from God as had been stated before and man in contradiction to God has good reason to feel him or herself threatened in his or her existence . It is therefore the consequence of the threat upon his or her disobedience "- "Thou shalt surely die." Gen 2 :17.

Judaism and Christianity both hold that man has a great potential for either goodness or evil. Existentialism on the other hand view a man as being in a perpetual process of becoming through continuous crisis. The basic problem is the variety of ideas and some contradictory which has come under its cloak. Existentialists therefore suggest a fresh way of looking at human existence.

Faith is certainly of conviction based on one's experience of thought and feeling, not assent to propositions on credit of the proposer. The prevailing mood is that of joy while the prevailing mood in Authoritarian religion is that of sorrow and guilt.

This life is not determined by our external circumstances such as how much money we have; who we know, where we work or by our marital status but rather the internal condition of our hearts. The difference between what we think is urgent and what really matters hence our lives are filled with things other people think are urgent for instance money; cars; clothes and so on but how often do we stop to think about what really matters in our lives.

We have let our lives be controlled by money. We have forgotten about dreams and visions but there is still time in our lives to change course by asking God to help restore in us His dreams and visions for our lives. We can build up our faith by praying in the Spirit.

We basically have two lives. We have an outer life which is our reputation with people and an inner life which is our reputation with God. We can be doing one thing on the outside and something totally different in the inside at the same time.

No matter how upsetting things may get around us, we can remain calm; cool and collected for instance, in a deep body of water like the Ocean. There can be a storm going on outside causing all sorts of waves on the surface but if you go down deep the water, it will be as still and quiet as if there was no storm at all.

To tap into the golden silence of God's peace, is to stop making excuses and accept the fact that, it is our responsibility to keep ourselves calm. If we choose to be controlled by God's Spirit which is peaceful and quiet, we will not be controlled by our stormy flesh. When we allow our emotions to be stirred up by unpleasant circumstances, we are in danger of missing the leading of God and being led by our feelings.

We were created to live with purpose and passion. It is what gets us up and keeps us going each day. God has placed in each of us a strong desire to reach for something beyond ourselves which is a natural longing to reach for the goals that are unreachable apart from His help. We were created to enjoy God and do His will because He is the Alpha and the Omega - the Beginning and the End, therefore He must also be everything in between. Knowing and understanding our purpose is the first step toward doing all God has planned for us. When we understand our purpose, it becomes a road map guiding us toward our destiny in Christ. Passion is the fuel that keeps us going on our journeys. Therefore, it is vital that we keep an ample supply and we should constantly be experiencing the life of God Who does everything passionately and with purpose with His whole heart.

God has given us hopes and dreams to pursue with our whole hearts. The problem is that many of us have the passion to see the things we hope for, because reality has been buried and we have given in hopelessness when it seemed like our dreams would never become reality.

I am stands for my nature; I can represent my capacities; I should or should not symbolize my value. I want stands for my inspiration of which all represent my various; my self - image; self - concept and self-structure which are used to describe our personality construct.

The higher Intelligence groups conduct their human relations as they would a game of Chess. For them, every move is more or less deliberately calculated 'My so-called "Enemies" are now playing a protective game. Why is it they are protecting. With God's Grace, *Ha ke le lle Nama*; *Ha ke le lle Masapo. Ke le lla Moya* meaning I am not crying for flesh; I am not crying for my bones. I am crying for my Soul.

When the behaviour and the basic philosophy of life are at odds, the personality usually is in trouble. A person's philosophy of life usually includes his or her beliefs about the origin and nature of truth; the purpose and significance of his or her particular life; the nature of reality including the possibility of a personal God which also includes the nature and the hierarchy of values he or she holds as well as the origin and destiny of man.

In my understanding, the unconscious beliefs are learned during the growing - up process from values held by parents and others close to the person. When a person is armed with the rationally derived knowledge and insight, he or she can proceed to the development of a trustworthy and unified self - system value structure which is no longer focused on external values. As a result, he or she should be no longer a blind slave to his or her core needs and values nor a victim of an externally imposed value system.

He or She need not depend heavily upon the ideas; feelings; people and objects about him or her since he or she now has a cohesive independent value structure uniquely his or her own because value is a form of conscious or unconscious belief in the worth of an idea or feeling.

Conscience connotes three quite different things which are: involuntary submission to external Authorities with the concomitant fear of discovery and punishment; condemnatory self - accusation and lastly discontent with self in a constructive sense.

The greatest human tragedy is to give up searching for the wide open and spacious life of which we are not fenced in. Instead we settle for mediocrity; routine; comfort and complacency. God wants us to be real through and through so that what people see on the outside is really who we are on the inside. (Mat, 23:25 -28).

Chapter 32

BITE THE BULLET AND FOLLOW YOUR HEART

It is therefore my job to search for and seek peace hence I realised that I would need to discover, what is stealing it from my life before I could find it. I pray and ask God to show me things that are allowing the Enemy to rob me of peace. The Enemy loves it when we live in the flesh; saying and doing all kinds of things based on how we feel.

If he or she can steal our peace, he or she knows that he or she can get us to do all kinds of things we will regret later and make wrong decisions that will lead to other problems. We all have an Eagle within, and Eagles use storms to gain momentum hence being okay without being perfect is what matters.

A wise person never accepts everything for what it appears to be because he or she has learned that appearances can be deceiving and he or she therefore examines things carefully. People without wisdom make hasty decisions and often do things they regret later.

When we submit to God, we are sowing seeds of obedience that will bring a wonderful harvest in our lives. I realised that; each time I have ignored the inside information thereafter I have been sorry later. I therefore plan and execute my first failure so that I no longer have to fear it.

According to James 4 – 6 which says: "We should pray and ask God to show us a plan for each day and begin to work the plan because waking up each morning and knowing that, we were born for this day; that we are living in the purpose of God and are part of the great adventure of expanding His Kingdom here on earth as it is in Heaven."

We can make a habit of following the leading of God's Spirit by keeping our inner man quiet when things around us become difficult or confusing. If we keep our Spirit quiet, then we can easily hear the voices of His Holy Spirit. God has not given us the ability to control all our circumstances, but He has given us the ability to control ourselves. (Gen 5: 22 - 23).

When difficulties and frustrating circumstances come my way, I see these bumps in the road as opportunities to believe in God. I love believing in God because He never let me down. He may not always answer in the way I expect but He will never let me down. I think, it is shame to let a day go by and not enjoying the gift of each twenty-four hours period. I therefore suggest that you too, be sure to enjoy today because you are never going to get this day back because God wants us to face our challenges in life and not run away from them.

In Romans2: 6 - 8, Paul describes clearly that some people are given the ability to manage and oversee things. Others have a gift to teach and lead; others have the ability to serve or give generously. This indicates that, each of us is equally important and together we make up the body of Christ, Jesus being the head hence the secret of success is to make your vocation your vocation.

No matter how disappointing or difficult life becomes, nothing can permanently prevent it from rising to the surface for instance, by pushing the beach ball under the surface of water, it will rise and float on water. As a result, the Psychological viewpoint is that the person must be helped to develop his or her own frame of value reference suited to his or her times with unique circumstances and needs.

According to Freudian view, Conscience is considered a learned concept arising largely out of internalisation; parental prohibitions; threats and values. These internalized values are picked up through the process of incidental learning during early childhood. Punishment rather than Rewards seem to be the decisive determinants. According to his framework, Personality problems are caused by severe superego overwhelming the ego and forcing it to repress the biologically based primitive impulses of the id.

Mowrer claims that disturbances in personality are caused by the id and the ego by joining forces against superego and that the ego functions are immature and under the influence of the id have done things of which the superego disapproves. In this sense, the person with a diminutive superego and an immature ego would tend toward antisocial criminal acts whereas the person with the overdeveloped superego would lead to over socialization and rigidly which would place severe demands on the ego and restraint on the id.

It is therefore said, the dual task of the Counsellor is to help the person to develop a stronger ego that can escape control by the id and to develop a working relationship with the superego. Many people try to do what someone else is good at instead of doing what they are good at. Unfortunately, most people do not take the time to ask themselves, why they do what they do. God in my understanding is less concerned or impressed by what we do than why we do it?

A humanistic view is that, if the child grows up feeling that Conscience is somewhat absolute and synonymous with divine or cosmic law. That child may go through life trying to live up to these expectations; justifying his or her actions and forever feeling guilty that he or she should be doing something he or she isn't doing or not doing something he or she is doing. Conscience can be a positive creative force in interpersonal relationships as well as an inhibiting guilt provoking force.

Is further said, as the child grows, parental demands become internalized into feelings of rightness and wrongness. When he or she grows into adolescence, he or she acquires a self-picture as a moral person with the mores which is part of his or her basic value system. This value system is based on earlier learned values; a growing self - awareness and rationally determined view of the mores.

The year 2012! How can someone be so heartless? Well it is said, before something great happens, something wrong happens. Come hell or high water. Did you ever wish you had never been born? It did to me because my bossy Employer who is cold hearted man and who cares more for position than any human being by feathering his nest at other people's expense. His optimism was soon justified by the outcomes of his evil deeds. He and his acquaintances have the wrong sow by the ear because I am not easily impressed.

I am talking about the case of the weak character yielding to the strong. Nothing could have been more exactly calculated to set up my back to the wall as a result they had me under their thumbs but I am ready to go all length to fight for my Rights; my Profession and for my Family. I think when things are at their worst , tomorrow will be better hence I wrote to you , informing you as well as legal teams of my circumstances due to the seed sown by him had borne fruit by losing no opportunity to get the better of me which made me realise that, under the façade lay a cold and calculating nature . I cannot blame my learner for succumbing to temptation in her circumstances and obliged to earn her bread. Has it occurred to her that my employer is placing her under his obligation?

Chapter 33

THIS IS NOT WHO I AM

Before a person can commit him or herself in marriage, did he or she ask him or herself, what is this man or woman like? Or what is the personality of this man or woman?

I am saying this because in my understanding, the Therapist doesn't tell the Couple how to run their lives as he or she does not function as an Arbitrator by telling the Couple who is right and who is wrong and he or she plays no favourites. He or she does not place a blame but he or she helps them to understand how others have solved similar problems, having worked through the unexpressed and unrecognised dependencies as a result their relationships improved. The Counsellor or Therapist often deal with the Spouse not involved in the infidelity. Referrals in marital counselling should be well informed about the problem and have direct contact with if needs be.

I discovered that, Marriage between healthy, self - actualizing people is a merging of feelings and intellectual choices and when the choice is felt to be right. Therefore, faulty sex education; not carefully used "sex manuals" approach can be grossly misleading or unhealthy sex attitudes learned in childhood are frequent sources of trouble.

In my opinion, Separation is the only means by which a marriage can be saved. Sometimes a Separation is a necessary transition to final divorce. Separation is seldom instigated by the Counsellor or Therapist because, transference feelings have their roots in the person's life experience as a result a guy or lady with no respect could get ideas and others have enough charm to calm a snake hence he or she died spiritually for unnatural sexual causes or offences and I was on the other side convicted; dismissed and sentenced for three years imprisonment for Unnatural Sexual

Offence which I did not commit and not even understand. Is asking a girl learner as class monitor for the deceased classmate's contributions paid to her by her classmates in our School as agreed and arranged and by mere using a Cell phone a crime this days?

Is it legal or fair to be accused of "Attempted rape ; Sexual indecency ; Sexual Assault and later Unnatural Sexual Offence as per their different charge sheets and hearsay statements for using a mere Cell phone without using sexual advances or with no intimate or sexual relationship messages or conversation and having no intimate or love relationship?

Investigators and Police detectives not investigating or questioning the matter first by finding the real reasons why she decided to send me a personalised "Please call "without being forced to do so. Not investigating what was the reason or call or conversation was all about and what led me to end up writing her messages and what the messages were all about? Not looking at one side of the story because I had the right to put forth my side of story and not to take sides as they did to me.

My so-called "Employer" and Police Detectives threating innocent learners who were not in the Scene and who saw nothing to be the witnesses and testify lies against me ; changing their statements to suit their needs or else they will expelled from School . They arrested me just because they failed to do their investigations. False information about me and the so-called "Victim" published on Newspapers before investigations of Labour and Court hearings and being still at work not knowing this issue which led me to all this situation, I found myself at present.

Is it legal to be threatened by a Bias Prosecutor before Court proceedings to admit guilty to get a suspended sentence even though I did not commit such a crime? Is it fair or correct for the Prosecutor to befriend and share jokes and laugh with my defence Attorney before proceedings? Is it legal for the same Prosecutor to lie to my defence Attorney and the Magistrate for the so-called "Victim and her Witnesses" for failing to appear in Court as scheduled? Is it legal for the same Prosecutor to convince my defence Attorney to shorten and quickly close the case as it has taken too long by not following the correct procedures and this was done behind my back?

The same Prosecutor was always intimidating me before Court's proceedings by asking and questioning as well as telling me about my defence Attorney's whereabouts; telling me about what he heard about my labour hearings which were still pending of which I was not aware of and by telling everyone before court's proceedings, how happy he was to see the so-called "Victim and her mother" and that he even lied to the Magistrate about their failure of attending court hearings.

Is it legal for the Prosecutor of telling me that I intended to sleep with the so-called "Victim "instead of asking relevant questions than twisting everything and oppressing me as a layman to be seen as a bad and be seen guilty for the crime I didn't commit?

Is it the correct procedure not to allow or give a chance the so-called complainant's witnesses who were threatened and forced to testify against me to be questioned of what they have seen or heard in their presence because the Prosecutor lied to my defence Attorney that they were not in Court on that specific day. Even the Police as State Witnesses did not testify in Court about their findings or investigations but only the mother of the so-called "Victim" who was not there and my former learner was given a chance to testify against me about what she heard from her daughter of what happened in class on that specific day.

On the other hand my defence Attorney never met with me to discuss the case before appearances in

Court except when they wanted me to sign the claim forms from Scorpion Legal Department of which I was the member, by always saying that I should not worry as there is no case at all and took my case lightly.

My witnesses who were there on the specific day who saw and talked with the so-called "Victim" before and after the so-called "Incident" in the School premises were not given the opportunity to testify on my behalf in both Labour and Court's proceedings in their presence. My evidences to prove my innocence were hidden and not used in both proceedings for instance, Newspaper Articles, Affidavit of my lost cell phone as well as my witnesses.

I am not happy and not satisfied about the way my so-called "Case" was handled from the start up to an end in both Labour and Court proceedings. Truthfully, there were no witnesses in my case, and no one knew what really happened on that specific day, only Hearsays were used to unfairly and wrongfully dismiss and convict as well as to sentence me, just for being a Teacher. It was just her word against mine.

CHAPTER 34

DISMISSED, RETRENCHED, CONVICTED. SUICIDAL THOUGHTS AND DEPRESSION! I AM SOUL PRECIOUS.

Love involves learning to give and receive love. The needs of the other must be at least as important as one's own otherwise mature love does not exist. Mature love requires spaces in your togetherness, stand together, yet not too near together for the Pillars of the Temple stand apart – the Oak tree and the Cypress grow not in each other's shadow.

To love someone because you need him or her is neurotic but to need him or her because you love him or her is healthy. We have common types of neurotic attraction which are, when one aggressive and sadistic versus one dependent and submissive. The oneself – sufficient through emotional detachment versus one extremely considerate, one with fluctuating helplessness and assertiveness versus one fluctuating in responsibility and disappointment desire for love and finally mutual attempt at domination.

Love in this sense is both an emotional feeling and a decision and must not be regarded as solely one or the other. The neurotic individual often seeks to establish intimacy with another by sexual contact rather through a gradual association. Experiences of sudden intimacy are usually short - lived and unsatisfying because, sexual desire is often mistaken with love. Frequently sexual desire is motivated by other neurotic needs of which are the anxiety of aloneness. The wish to conquer or to be conquered. Vanity and the wish to hurt or even to destroy.

I therefore suggest that, each individual must discover what love means and how a person can become lovable and loving in his or her own way because the affirmation of that person, meaning granting him or her gladly the full right to his or her unique manhood.

Romantic love has cultural roots in the past, but it survives in the present and nurtured by an endless barrage of fairy tales told in myriads of slightly different forms in movies, magazines, TVs, and novels. Caring, on the other hand, is expressed as a way of manifesting love and mature love comes only after a knowledge of and experience with the loved partner. It may follow a period of disillusionment associated with romantic love.

There are several basic elements of mature love of which are, the active concern for the life and growth of that which we love, responsibility for the needs, physical and psychic of the other, respect for the other, the ability to see a person as he or she is. To be aware of his or her unique individuality and knowledge of self as well as of the other and of the nature of love.

One falls out of love because one does not work through the period of disillusionment to a new conception of love based not on projected needs but on realistic appraisal of one another and a deep valuing of each other as unique persons.

Counterfeit love on the other hand can be recognised when the relationship is degrading, exploitive, violent, antisocial, irresponsible, sadistic, or masochistic. Love between man and woman is a relationship in which each helps the other to preserve and enlarge the life of the other.

For me, love gives naught but itself and takes naught but from itself. Love possesses not nor would be possessed, for love is sufficient unto love. We are to live passionate life; we must first understand the difference between passion and obligation. From passion, you do what you want but from a sense of obligation, you do what you must.

It was passion that motivated me to ask Bella out on a date. No one forced me to do it. I was fuelled by the force of passion and it worked because I did not only get a date with her, I got a lovely honest and beautiful wife. That proves, you do what you want from passion, therefore we should not settle for a mere existence but pursue the passionate and abundant life that Jesus came to give us.

I discovered that, things in life often start out as a passion but end up by becoming a boring obligation. That faith starts with passion and then becomes a ritual. Marriages begin with passion and become a boring routine. That ministry starts with passion and ends up as an obligation.

When we live with passion, we honour God powerfully because He created us with passion and loves us with a passion. If we are to reflect the image of our Creator, we ought to be passionate people.

I realised that, some of us are only passionate about spiritual matters like church, Bible study or Christian events but not about our families, marriages, work, leisure, or hobbies. Yes! It is wonderful to be passionate about our Spiritual life, but something is wrong if that is the only area where passion is applied.

Paul wrote: “Whatever you do, do it heartily.” This applies to every area of our lives including those things we are not gifted to do. Those things we are commanded to do and those things we are called to do.

In my understanding, every man dies but not every man really lives because we can look great on the outside but if we are worried and anxious on the inside, we are not glorifying God. The wide-open spacious life that Paul spoke about in 2 Corinthians 6:11 – 13 can only be fuelled by the force of passion because it is internally regulated by the Spirit of God and not externally motivated by events or circumstances.

The passion I am talking about is the way you and I approach life, not sexual intimacy or bursts of emotion that come and go. It is time to forsake hopelessness and unbury old hopes and dreams. It is time to determine that, we will fulfil the purpose God has for us with His zeal to walk in the plans He has for us by enjoying everyday life.

I suggest that, we should be like an Olympic athlete who has an inner force of passion that drives him or her to sacrifice. Stay focused and stay committed. It is passion that has motivated an Athlete to get out of bed and train when everyone else is asleep because passion drove him or her to a disciplined life. So, could we.

I therefore encourage you and I to pursue being all we can be. To draw closer to God and discover our specific calling in life. Once you know it, stay focused, give yourself to your gift and do it passionately.

While one person hesitates because he or she feels inferior, the other is busy making mistakes and becoming superior hence my destiny is to do more. Teach more and reach more people.

I believe a good mother is not a bully and my so-called "victim's" mother is still bitter about the past as a school learner. She insulted me like I fell from the trees as a result in a twist of fate, I was dismissed from work and taken to prison for wrong reasons, but I believe that, later people will see me as a valuable asset.

For me, publicity is evil because I have a soft spot for education. I do not like to mix business with pleasure as that is a recipe for disaster. The proof of pudding is in the eating because violence breeds violence therefore it is not a walk in the Park. I am a dead man walking these days. I don't like being on the back foot like these as my colleagues and friends chose to cut and run as a result I was put in a hospice where when you cross the line, you get punished. Oh Gosh! That was a last straw to spite me because to them I was like a mosquito buzzing around their heads.

Well! I have poetry to pen and drama to create to take my mind off things as I was stabbed in the back because wherever they are , there are always fireworks and they chewed my ear off by choosing big bucks over love forgetting that, more money, more problems . I had to do what had to be done as it said, grizzly bear can detect the smell of its prey a mile away, despite its size, and it is fast. You do not want to meet it in the forest. They have turned my heart into stone by playing dirty by being no-good two-faced cows even though I tried to clear the air between us.

It is said, tattoos have now become mainstream in modern societies, however according to a research, people with tattoos seem to be more aggressive and rebellious and that every important decision has repercussions. People should try and look objective. Fear for me is a powerful weapon and that, respect on the other hand is earned, not demanded.

I think we are in the same boat even though too many cooks spoil the broth. By so saying, I am not sticking my nose in other people's business and I am not the man who thinks on his feet hence I believe that all this will pass. Small legacy was all that my beloved deceased parents could leave me are a world map and two pistols meaning they left me the world and the weapons to conquer it. May their Souls rest in Peace! With Love and Gratitude!

CPSIA information can be obtained
at www.ICGtesting.com
Printed in the USA
LVHW081344221222
735718LV00014B/614

9 781990 988707